"These pages are filled with such helpful honesty and gospel centrality as we're invited to look at the wonderful and messy world of motherhood! Reading it was like opening a window in the stuffy room of pretense, guilt, and self-focus that often press in on us as mothers. Let the windows fly open and come breathe the fresh air of grace!"

Kristyn Getty, hymnwriter; recording artist

"As mothers, our to-do lists are never ending, and many well-meaning people pile on how-to lists to try to help us manage it all. Here's good news: *Treasuring Christ When Your Hands Are Full* refreshes the soul with gospel truths and is not a how-to book. Gloria Furman shares the liberating gospel on every page, helping us fix our eyes on eternity rather than on our circumstances. You won't come away with yet another thing to do; instead you'll know the one who gave it all for you and has much to say in his word to sustain you."

Trillia Newbell, author, *If God Is for Us: The Everlasting Truth of Our Great Salvation*

"Moms do not need another book telling them how short they fall or what they can do to 'be a better parent.' Moms need a book that will lift their eyes away from themselves and onto Christ. Gloria Furman has delivered just that book. Her honesty about her daily struggles and her hope in her strong Savior are a delightful encouragement. The grand picture of God and his redeeming love that Gloria paints gives courage to face each day. We will be recommending this book to future moms, new moms, and moms that have been at it for years."

Jessica Thompson and Elyse Fitzpatrick, coauthors, *Give Them Grace*

"Oh, how I wish I had had a voice like Gloria Furman's to whisper such sweet gospel truths into the frustrations and discontent of my younger mothering days! There's nothing simplistic or syrupy here. This book presents rich and deep wisdom that is sure to generate joy and peace in the homes and hearts of many moms."

Nancy Guthrie, Bible teacher; author, *Seeing Jesus in the Old Testament* Bible study series

"A stunning invitation to see Christ in and through the everyday mundane. Every mother needs to read this book, to bathe her soul in the truth of the gospel, to 'stamp eternity on her eyeballs,' and then come back tomorrow and do it all again. This book should sit on every nightstand of every weary mother wondering if there is anything more to look forward to than another sink full of dirty dishes, another day full of cleaning and wiping, cooking and scrubbing. The answer Gloria points us to is Jesus. And he is more than enough. I will be buying this book by the case and giving it away to all the moms I meet!"

Joy Forney, missionary; wife and mother; blogger

"I was wonderfully blessed by this book. With personal examples and teaching immersed in Scripture, Gloria invites us to savor Christ, the deepest need and joy of every mother. I certainly will reread it and look forward to recommending it to others."

Trisha DeYoung, wife to Kevin DeYoung, author of *The Biggest Story Bible Storybook*

"We need this book. In the frenetic and sometimes overwhelming task of parenting, it's hard to remember the gospel. Thank God for Gloria Furman! She helps us worship Jesus in the midst of chaotic commotion and see 'interruptions' as invitations to joyfully trust him. Both mothers and fathers will find deep encouragement here."

Jon and Pam Bloom, President, Desiring God, and his wife

Treasuring Christ When Your Hands Are Full

Also by Gloria Furman:

Glimpses of Grace: Treasuring the Gospel in Your Home (2013)

The Pastor's Wife: Strengthened by Grace for a Life of Love (2015)

Word-Filled Women's Ministry: Loving and Serving the Church (2015)

Missional Motherhood: The Everyday Ministry of Motherhood in the Grand Plan of God (2016)

Alive in Him: How Being Embraced by the Love of Christ Changes Everything (2017)

Joyfully Spreading the Word: Sharing the Good News of Jesus (2018)

Labor with Hope: Gospel Meditations on Pregnancy, Childbirth, and Motherhood (2019)

Treasuring Christ When Your Hands Are Full

Gospel Meditations for Busy Moms

Gloria Furman

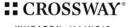

CROSSWAY®

WHEATON, ILLINOIS

Treasuring Christ When Your Hands Are Full: Gospel Meditations for Busy Moms
© 2014, 2024 by Gloria C. Furman

Published by Crossway
    1300 Crescent Street
    Wheaton, Illinois 60187

Published in association with the literary agency of Wolgemuth & Associates, Inc.

Cover design: Erik Maldre & Crystal Courtney

Cover image: Brandon Hill Photos, BrandonHillPhotos.com

First printing 2014

Reprinted with study questions 2024

Printed in the United States of America

Trade paperback ISBN: 978-1-4335-9364-2
ePub ISBN: 978-1-4335-3891-9
PDF ISBN: 978-1-4335-3889-6

Library of Congress Cataloging-in-Publication Data

Furman, Gloria, 1980–
Treasuring Christ when your hands are full : gospel meditations for busy moms / Gloria Furman.
pages cm
Includes bibliographical references and index. ISBN 978-1-4335-3888-9 (tp)
1. Mothers—Religious life. 2. Spirituality—Christianity.
Title.
BV4529.18.F87   2014
248.8'431—dc23   2013037994

Crossway is a publishing ministry of Good News Publishers.

VP		33	32	31	30	29	28	27	26	25	24
15	14	13	12	11	10	9	8	7	6	5	4	3	2	1

To my mother, Catherine

Contents

Acknowledgments

THANK YOU, *JESUS*, for building your church here in the Middle East. Thank you to *the older women at Redeemer Church of Dubai*, who take the instructions in Titus 2 seriously. You dote on the babes in Christ, instruct younger women, and teach what is good. Thank you for your faithful "mothering" as you exhort and encourage women to love their families and adorn the gospel. You're a blessing to me and so many! Thank you, *Cheryl Madewell*, for the countless hours you spent with me when I was a sophomore in college, teaching me to put great effort into studying and loving God's word. Thank you, *Ngoc Brown* and *Carolyn Wellons*, for teaching me that I need to treasure Christ in order to love my pastor-husband. Thank you, *Mary Waters*, for showing how the joy of the Lord is our strength to care for people through seasons of suffering. Thank you, *Kim Blough*, for sitting with me in that dark season in the desert when I felt that my hands would only ever be full of pain and hopelessness. You held out the hope of the gospel to me over and over again—thank you.

I'm thankful for these bloggers who specifically write and blog in order to point mothers to treasure Christ. Thank you for your friendship and sharpening influence, *Lindsey Carlson*, *Kimm Crandall*, *Christina Fox*, *Trillia Newbell*, *Luma Simms*, and *Jessica Thompson*.

It is a precious thing to have friends who pursue Christ through all the delights and sorrows of motherhood. Thank you, *Monica deGarmeaux* and *Laurie Cuchens*, for modeling this to me through both profound grief and joy. By God's grace, your lives testify that the God whom you worship is worthy of all praise.

Thank you to the team at *Crossway* (especially *Justin Taylor*, *Lydia Brownback*, *Josh Dennis*, *Amy Kruis*, *Angie Cheatham*, and *Janni Firestone*) for all the energy and hard work that was put into this book.

A huge thank you to my mom, *Catherine*, and my mother-in-law, *Basia*, who even from over eight thousand miles away find ways to creatively love and encourage our family.

Introduction

Stamp Eternity on My Eyeballs

MY HANDS WERE ALREADY FULL when I was pregnant with our first child.

They were full with books, jars, door handles, shower knobs, chairs, steering wheels, buttons, forks, and keyboards.

It was when I was pregnant with our first child that my husband began to suffer from chronic pain due to a nerve disorder in both of his arms. In a rather short period of time the stabbing, burning pain greatly restricted what Dave was able to do with his arms. "It's amazing how much you need your arms," Dave remarked one evening as I was hunched over my nine-months-pregnant belly helping him wrestle his socks on and tie his shoes. At that time we had very little idea of what his nerve disease would mean for our daily lives as parents. It's been nearly eight years since his initial electric-like pains began. Over the years he has had multiple surgical procedures, and he's still in pain. Dave describes it as a sort of "white noise."

A couple years ago, Dave got an infection that developed into a large boil on top of the nerves in his hand. Boils are a common affliction where we live in the Middle East, according to the doctors at the hospital where Dave was treated. He was hospitalized for three days as they took special care to rescue his hand. "What's it like to be married to Job?" Dave joked as he was discharged from the hospital. It was good to see him smiling despite this ordeal. I was reminded of Job's declaration of faith: "Though he slay me, I will hope in him" (Job 13:15). And I was sobered by the poor demonstration of the faith of Job's wife, who said, "Do you still hold fast your integrity? Curse God and die" (Job 2:9). The impact of my godly, long-suffering husband has been a key influence in my motherhood.

Even against the backdrop of pain, I see abundant evidence of the grace of God at work in our lives. Through daily troubles we have opportunities to testify that "the steadfast love of the Lord never ceases; his mercies never come to an end" (Lam. 3:22).

I wanted to share that piece of my life with you because it has shaped my perspective on what it means to physically and emotionally have "your hands full." Having more physical work in motherhood than I had anticipated forces me to look to the Lord for strength and provision. I'm learning firsthand how turning to the world for comfort and strength just leaves me dissatisfied and weak. God has used our family's physical circumstances to point me to the one great permanent circumstance in my life—the gospel of Jesus Christ. I'm eager to share more about this with you and how it relates to motherhood.

My hands are full with hard work, helping my husband, and raising our four children. Your hands are full too, even if your circumstances as a mom are different from mine. In our cross-cultural work we've been privileged to travel the world, and now we live in a global city where people from over one hundred nationalities live together. Mothers are a diverse lot, but I think the statement is universally true—a mother's hands are always full.

But what are they filled with?

Sometimes my playful son hands me boogers or indiscernible food matter from under his high chair as a present. My girls hand me cryptic notes saturated through with glitter pens. It's part of my job as their mother to accept these love offerings with cheer (and sometimes hand sanitizer).

The old saying contains truth: "A mother's work is never done." As mothers go about their day caring for their children, they might physically carry them, gather random dishes from around the house, work to help provide for their children, pull squabbling siblings apart, turn pages in storybooks, and push the vacuum over trodden popcorn.

Mothers also have their hands full with hugs and high-fives. It could go without saying that many times a day (or hour!), a mother might also wring her hands in frustration and lift up her hands in prayer as she cries out to God for help.

Whatever you feel that your hands are filled with—blessings or difficulties or a comingling of both—God's word contains specific encouragement for you.

There is more to be said about a mother's work than the fact that it is hard and that it is never done. There is beauty and brilliance and God-given dignity to a mother's work. I'll talk about some of those things in this book.

But what I'm most concerned with communicating in these limited pages is that mothers can appreciate an even greater reality than the fact of their role as mothers. It doesn't matter where you are from or what your circumstances are; the greatest reality a mother can appreciate and rest in is the work that Jesus has done on the cross on our behalf.

- Jesus's purifying and cleansing work through the blood sacrifice of his own body on the cross is preeminent over the dirty laundry that is threatening an avalanche soon.

- Jesus's victorious rising from the dead and triumph over death are preeminent over the chaos of your busy household as everyone is shuttled off to where they need to be for the day.
- Jesus's sovereign reign over the cosmos and eschatological harnessing of everything under his feet are preeminent over the plans you've made for the evening, your busy schedule this weekend, and the ideas you have about your child's future.

The Christian mother's hands are full with every spiritual blessing in Christ (Eph. 1:3), and her work in nurturing children in the fear of the Lord is her privileged participation in God's work in uniting all things in Jesus (Eph. 1:10). This Jesus, whom we gladly serve, offers rest to mothers and fills our hands with his blessings. Day and night, moment by moment, we must choose to rest in Jesus. That's what it means to treasure Christ when your hands are full, whether you have one child or a dozen.

A mother who has been born again to a living hope through the resurrection of Christ has an inheritance that is imperishable, undefiled, and unfading, kept in heaven for her (1 Pet.

1:3–4). Even as a mother's hands can be filled with troubles, back-breaking work, and frightening unknowns, she is being guarded by God's power through faith for a salvation to be revealed in the future (1 Pet. 1:5). Because of the gospel, we mothers can rejoice as we find our hands full of blessings in Jesus, because all we know is grace. Theologian Herman Bavinck said that based on Jesus's sacrifice for our sins on the cross, "God can wrench the world and humanity out of the grip of sin and expand his kingdom."[1] This is very, *very* good news.

I need to be reminded of this news all the time, dozens of times a day. I need reminders because I can defend and announce a biblical theology of God's grace to mothers yet still not live in the identity and hope that God gives me.

The Good News for Every Day

Jonathan Edwards used to pray and ask that God would "stamp eternity on my eyeballs." This prayer has become my own heart's request too.

When your eyes are fixed on the horizon of eternity, it affects your vision for motherhood. We need to have eyes to see a view of God that is so big and so glorious that it transforms our perspective of motherhood. In the context of eternity, where Christ is doing his work of reigning over the cosmos, we need to see our mundane moments for what they really are—worship. In the daily (and nightly) work of mothering, we're given dozens of invitations to worship God as he reminds us of the hope we have because of his gospel. My prayer is that you would see that the gospel is good news for mothers, not just on our "born again birthday," but every single day.

The ministry of the Holy Spirit includes bringing our subjective insecurities as mothers in line with the objective reality of our eternal security in Christ. As mothers we need to train ourselves to focus on the things that are unseen and eternal (2 Cor. 4:18). As we struggle to maintain this perspective *and* even as we fail to struggle, relenting to the temptation toward apathy, we must look to God's word and believe it, even when we can't feel it. We need to be women of God's word whose daily petition is: "Teach me your way, O Lord, that I may walk in your truth; unite my heart to fear your name" (Ps. 86:11). As we walk in God's truth, we also sense the Spirit's invitations to pray. Although written to pastors, Martyn Lloyd-Jones's words on prayer are relevant to us:

> Always respond to every impulse to pray. Where does it come from? It is the work of the Holy Spirit (Phil.

2:12–13). . . . So never resist, never postpone it, never push it aside because you are busy. . . . Such a call to prayer must never be regarded as a distraction; always respond to it immediately, and thank God if it happens to you frequently.[2]

A mother's work is holy unto the Lord.

As mothers we look to Jesus not only as our example; we also see that he is our power to love God and our children. Because Christ has done for us what we could never do for ourselves, with *his* power we can ask forgiveness of our children when we sin against them, because God in Christ has forgiven us (Matt. 6:12–15; Mark 11:25; Col. 3:13). With *his* power we can humble ourselves in our work as mothers, because no one ever displayed more humility than our Redeemer as he abandoned his right to stay in heaven and died the death we deserve (Phil. 2:3–8). With *his* power we can pursue our family with sacrificial love, because the Son gladly submitted to the Father's will (John 14:30–31). And even when we fail to love as he loves, he is our righteousness. Jesus has done for us what we could never do for ourselves. Jesus is our anchor, and he has anchored us in his love; nothing, nothing, *nothing* will ever separate us from the love of God in Christ Jesus our Lord (Rom. 8:39).

The gospel stands above and beyond all the most practical, family-friendly, or cost-effective philosophies of mothering. The good news of Jesus Christ is superior to our to-do lists and metaphorical mother-of-the-year trophies. This is because the greatest problem a mother has is not a lack of creativity, accomplishment, or skill, but her inability to love God and others as Jesus loves her (John 13:34). Without a mediator to speak for us, our sin will surely separate us from our holy God, both now and forever (Rom. 3:23). If you've never been alarmed by that idea and subsequently comforted by the cross of Jesus Christ, then I encourage you—please keep reading.

Treasuring Christ When Your Hands Are Full is not a to-do list on how to be a good mother. It's about our good God and what he has done. God's irresistible grace binds our wandering hearts to himself and frees us to love him back and overflow in love to our neighbors. We have been ransomed from sin and death and given eternal life by the precious blood of Christ (1 Pet. 1:18–19). And because of Christ's work on the cross, we can live God's way of love in our homes and in the world even as our hands are full (Gal. 5:16–26; Eph. 4:17–6:18).

While I do not venture to give sage advice in the how-to's of mothering (my oldest child is still in primary school), the application of the gospel to motherhood is immensely practical. I kept a note on my desktop while writing these pages. The note says: "Resist the urge to reduce God's word to nice tips for nice living: give them the gospel."[3] Bible-based tips never rescued anyone's soul from destruction or carried along the whispers of eternal life into their mundane. Jesus saves, and the fruit of the Spirit is far sweeter than the fruitless flowers of mere moral living. God transforms us from the inside out. As Puritan Jeremiah Burroughs aptly put it, "Contentment is a sweet, inward heart-thing. It is a work of the Spirit indoors."[4]

The circumstances of your motherhood may be difficult, troublesome, and confusing. Even so, there is a circumstance that supersedes all the complexities of your life. It is the simple truth that the one great, permanent circumstance in which you live is that you have been allowed to walk in newness of life as you are united to Christ by faith through grace. Our joy cannot be wrapped up in motherhood but only in God. All of us need to allow the Spirit to do his "indoor work" and marvel as the Lord cultivates sweet, inward contentment in our heart as we learn to trust him.

Perhaps you woke up before the sun today so you could enjoy fellowship with the Lord and get some work done, and now the day feels like it is just dragging on. I'm with you. I don't know how many times I've wondered: "Is it bedtime yet?" On days like this we need to remember that each day is like a sigh that is too brief to measure, yet it is chock full of eternal significance. And into this brief sigh of an ordinary day, the Holy Spirit erupts and overflows with the love of God in Christ into our heart. This is astonishing. Jesus invites us into something far more steadfast and indestructible than the things of this world. Believe it or not, there is something infinitely more permanent than the purple marker that your child used to decorate your ivory-colored kitchen cabinets. Because of his love, Jesus invites us to himself. He says in John 15:9, "As the Father has loved me, so have I loved you. Abide in my love."

It is my prayer that what you find in this book points you to treasure Christ as he has filled your hands with the good work of mothering. I need to remember these things, too, so these gospel meditations could also be one long "note to self." By God's grace would he refresh our hearts and renew our minds through his word and his Spirit that we would marvel at "the excellencies of him who called you out of darkness into his marvelous light" (1 Pet. 2:9).

Reflection

The Christian mother's hands are full with every spiritual blessing in Christ. "A mother's work is never done," the old saying goes. Much joy is found in the process of raising children, but we must admit that the joy is often tinged by frustration and exhaustion. The realities of motherhood can make us feel that we must shelve spiritual growth and the riches of God's kingdom until we reach a different season of life. But that's not the way it has to be. In fact, the very challenges inherent in motherhood are actually God's instruments for bringing forth spiritual growth and kingdom riches.

1. I have been frank about the suffering that my husband, Dave, and I have experienced through his illness, yet the suffering has strengthened, not weakened, my faith, and we have been able to testify to the truth of Lamentations 3:22: "The steadfast love of the Lord never ceases; his mercies never come to an end." How does suffering, more than anything else, provide an opportunity to learn this truth?

2. "God has used our family's physical circumstances to point me to the one great permanent circumstance in my life—the gospel of Jesus Christ." How does 2 Corinthians 1:3–6 explain how this is worked out in the lives of all who belong to God through Jesus Christ?

3. How do Ephesians 1:3–10 and 1 Peter 1:3–5 provide an eternal perspective on the ceaseless and sometimes monotonous tasks of motherhood?

4. Jonathan Edwards prayed, "Stamp eternity on my eyeballs." How does cultivating an eternal perspective help with motherhood (see pp. 6–8)?

5. Jesus is our power to love God and our children. How does that work out in practical ways (see pp. 8–9)?

Going Deeper

No one gladly chooses suffering, but no one escapes it either. And when it comes, we have a choice. We can try to deny it or escape it or tough it out like a stoic, or we can turn to God in faith and trust his divine governing of the details of our lives. Denial or escape or stoicism are the defaults of mankind. It's only through Scripture that we can learn how to profit from suffering. How do the following passages enable us to build a theology of suffering: Romans 5:1–5; 2 Corinthians 12:7–10; 1 Peter 4:12–13; James 1:2–4?

PART 1

GOD MADE MOTHERHOOD FOR HIMSELF

1

Hands Full of Blessings

A FEW YEARS AGO our family was blessed to live in the upstairs bedrooms of a villa that housed our church offices and community space. There was always something exciting going on downstairs, whether it was youth group, Bible study, or a world-class international church potluck. Even though people were in and out of our house all day and night, sometimes I got cabin fever. I got an itch to just get out of the house.

Thankfully, we lived down the street from a large shopping mall, so I could get out of the house (and avoid the sweltering desert heat). Sometimes I packed up the kids and took them window shopping, and I passed it off as an educational experience. "How many plates do you see stacked on this display table?" "Let's make up a story about the models wearing winter coats." "Who can spot the least expensive dress in this storefront?"

When I take my kids out to a public place like the mall, I become a sort of cat herder. (Can cats even be herded?) "Stay here with Mommy." "Don't touch that!" "Where did you pick *that* up? It doesn't belong in your mouth." "No scratching each other; only gentle hand-holding." "Giddy-up, keep moving, folks."

One time I was corralling my kittens into their seats at a table in the food court when a lovely woman sat down next to us.

There are hardly any "strangers" where we live, and the hospitality is impeccable. Hospitality extends beyond the living room as people cheerfully involve themselves in others' lives as they go about their day. Their sense of community extends far beyond their personal friends. The African adage "It takes a village to raise a child" is not just a saying where I live but an honored, normative reality. Sometimes it seems that the camaraderie of merely sharing space in a line at the ATM is enough to facilitate community among people.

"You have your hands full!" our lunch companion beamed as she laid her hand on my younger daughter's blond curls. "So beautiful! Mashallah" (Arabic for "God bless her").

It used to bother me when people said that my hands were full.

Because I'm self-conscious and insecure, I would take these comments as an affront to my ability to parent my children well. I assumed that people who said this were implying that my children were ill-mannered and wild and that I had no idea how to raise them, that my hands were full because I didn't have a handle on my careening, out-of-control motherhood. When I heard this comment, I would get defensive and haughty (and sometimes this is still a temptation).

Now, whenever someone tells me that I have my hands full, I agree with them for two reasons. The first reason I agree with people who say that my hands are full is that ninety-nine times out of one hundred, people mean that I *literally* have my hands full.

"Let me help you with that." The friendly woman stood up to take the tray I was holding as I attempted with my ankle to pull the baby's stroller closer to the table.

Second, I agree with people who say my hands are full, because my hands are not just full. They're *overflowing*—with blessings.

When people tell me that my hands are full, it's a good time to remember that it's true. "Yes! My hands are overflowing with God's gifts!"

The abundance of gifts that God has given me through motherhood is not quantifiable by the number of children I have or how delightful they are to me. The gifts that God has given mothers cannot be contained or quantified by their children.

Every Mother Has Her Hands Full

There is real trouble, real discouragement, and real back-breaking work that comes with motherhood. To say "Being a mom isn't easy" is like saying "Chocolate is yummy." This much is obvious. Just watch a mom who is nine months pregnant try to get out of a car and not pull any muscles in the attempt. Just listen to a mom share the aches in her heart for the child she is waiting to adopt. Or ask a mother to tell you her prayer requests. Being a mom isn't easy.

But sometimes mothers feel that their hands are full of inconvenience, thankless work, and futility. Maintaining the perspective that God has abundantly blessed you is a very real struggle. The fight for faith cannot be waged with the whimsical idea that you just need to see that "the glass is half full." The fight for faith should be addressed with sensitivity and grace and always subjected to the inerrant and authoritative word of God.

I know that struggles, disappointments, and pain in motherhood are significant issues, so it is with all seriousness and sincerity that I remind myself what the apostle Peter says in 1 Peter 1:3–5: I have been born again to a living hope through the resurrection of Christ, and I have an inheritance that is imperishable, undefiled, and unfading, kept in heaven for me. Even as my life is full of heartaches and triumphant victories, unknowns and hopes, I am being guarded by God's power through faith for a salvation to be revealed in the future. Preaching the gospel to myself each day is the best way to remind myself that my life in Christ is *the* prevailing, permanent reality in my life. The indwelling Holy Spirit comforts my soul with the truths of God's word.

When Jesus rescued me from hell, he also rescued me to himself. I have been spared an eternity of the just punishment that I deserve and have been handed life forever with my Savior. He took that cup—filled to the brim with the wrath of God against sin—and he drank it to the dregs. Then he didn't hand me back an empty cup (which itself would have been a mercy of unspeakable worth).[5] The Bible says that my glass isn't merely half full. Because of Jesus, our cup is filled to overflowing with God's blessings (Ps. 23:5).

I know that I may not be rescued from the next blowout diaper that leaks onto the floorboard of my car while I'm stuck in traffic with whining children who just want to get out and play. But because of the gospel I am rescued from having to respond to those troubles in the way my sinful flesh would prefer—I am strengthened by grace because I've been given the righteousness of Jesus Christ when I *do* respond sinfully. Because of the gospel I can also see God's good intentions to fulfill his promises to me in making me like Christ and drawing me nearer to himself. These are just a few of the ways the rubber meets the road when considering the gospel in daily life as a mom.

How does the gospel of Jesus Christ impact your life in a significant way when your seasonal reality seems to be absorbed by mundane things like bodily-fluid accidents and temper tantrums at the grocery store?

Anyone can advise you on how to deal with these practical, tangible things. For example, someone could suggest that you buy a poncho and wear it until your children are in junior high. To stifle your public temper tantrums, perhaps you could go into a closet and tantrum your temper in private. Oh? You thought I meant your *kid's* temper tantrum in the grocery store? Well, that's a different thing altogether!

Even if your first child has only just been conceived in your womb, or if you've recently been approved for an adoption, you can already taste the goodness of God to you in motherhood.

When I view motherhood *not* as a gift from God to make me holy but rather as a role with tasks that get in my way,

I am missing out on one of God's ordained means of spiritual growth in my life. Not only that, but I am missing out on *enjoying God*. No amount of mommy angst can compare to the misery that comes from a life devoid of the comforting, encouraging, guarding, providing, satisfying presence of our holy God.

I want for myself what Paul wanted for his beloved Philippians: "What you have learned and received and heard and seen in me—practice these things, and the God of peace will be with you" (Phil. 4:9). I want God's peace to rule my motherhood.

I want for myself what the writer of Hebrews wanted for his readers: "Strive for peace with everyone, and for the holiness without which no one will see the Lord" (Heb. 12:14). I want to live each day in the way that I learned Christ—that is, by grace through faith. I need to put off the old self, being renewed in the spirit of my mind, and put on the new self that is created after the likeness of God in true righteousness and holiness (Eph. 4:20–24). John Owen commented on the role of the gospel in this pursuit: "What then is holiness? Holiness is nothing but the implanting, writing, and living out of the gospel in our souls (Eph. 4:24)."[6]

This life of grace-infused faith would do wonders for the way I parent my children, of course, but what's more, it keeps my gaze fixed on God. It could be said that the most loving command in the Bible is this one:

> Go on up to a high mountain,
>   O Zion, herald of good news;
> lift up your voice with strength,
>   O Jerusalem, herald of good news;
>   lift it up, fear not;
> say to the cities of Judah,
>   "*Behold your God!*" (Isa. 40:9)

I want to be counted among those who "will see the Lord." I want to behold my God!

Gifts with a Holy Purpose

The gifts that God gives us serve this holy purpose—to direct our praise to the giver of those gifts. If you enjoy the gift of your children and the gift of your motherhood, but your joy terminates in those gifts, then you've missed the point of the gifts.

The gift of motherhood points mothers to treasure Jesus Christ as he transforms our hearts from the inside out.

That's the subject I am going to unpack in this book. In case you're too busy to read the rest of it (I know what that's like!), the gist of my thesis is this:

Because of the gospel—the news about what Jesus did on the cross to save sinners—mothers who make Christ their treasure can rejoice in their work as God works in them.

Because of Jesus, all a Christian knows is grace upon grace upon grace. By God's grace, our hands are filled to overflowing according to his riches in Christ Jesus. These riches include the fruit of the Holy Spirit—love, joy, peace, patience, kindness, goodness, faithfulness, gentleness, and self-control (Gal. 5:22–23). Mothers "who belong to Christ Jesus have crucified the flesh with its passions and desires" (Gal. 5:24). Mothers who live by the Holy Spirit should also keep in step with him (Gal. 5:25). So, as Paul exhorts us, "Let us not become conceited, provoking one another, envying one another" (Gal. 5:26). We should pursue peace with one another instead, and build one another up in our most holy faith. Even these manifestations of the fruit of the Spirit aren't an end in themselves. When God goes about his work of making us holy, he has an end in mind—our glorification together with Christ Jesus.

Read Romans 8:12–17 with yourself in mind. "So then, . . ."

So then, brothers, we are debtors, not to the flesh, to live according to the flesh. For if you live according to the flesh you will die, but if by the Spirit you put to death the deeds of the body, you will live. For all who are led by the Spirit of God are sons of God. For you did not receive the spirit of slavery to fall back into fear, but you have received the Spirit of adoption as sons, by whom we cry, "Abba! Father!" The Spirit himself bears witness with our spirit that we are children of God, and if children, then heirs—heirs of God and fellow heirs with Christ, provided we suffer with him in order that we may also be glorified with him.

Yes, mother, your hands are full, literally. And your hands are filled to overflowing with grace by the one who stretched his hands out for you on the cross.

———

Reflection

Maintaining the perspective that God has abundantly blessed you is a very real struggle. In this chapter I declared my thesis: "Because of the gospel—the news about what Jesus did on the cross to save sinners—mothers who make Christ their treasure can rejoice in their work as God works in them." The gospel is powerful. It has power to transform our lives because it first transforms our hearts. As we grow in our understanding of what Christ did on the cross, we will find ourselves treasuring our Savior more fully, thereby putting everything else we value into more fruitful perspective.

1. I used to get irritated when people pointed out the obvious—my hands are full. The comment made me feel as though I wasn't doing a good job as a mother. What caused my reaction, and how has my perspective changed (p. 19)? On which end of that spectrum would you place yourself today?

2. How would you answer the question: "How does the gospel of Jesus Christ impact your life in a significant way when your seasonal reality seems to be absorbed by mundane things like bodily-fluid accidents and temper tantrums at the grocery store?" How did I answer that question for my own life (p. 22)?

3. What perspective on motherhood can hinder our enjoyment of God? Conversely, what perspective enhances our enjoyment of both God and motherhood (pp. 22–24)?

4. God's gifts are meant to direct our praise to the giver of those gifts (p. 24). Do you view motherhood as a gift? Why or why not? How does your viewpoint impact your view of God?

5. God's goal in giving us children is to make us holy, which will eventually result in our glorification together with Christ. How does Romans 8:12–17 speak to you personally regarding your calling?

Going Deeper

Work your way through Galatians 5, noting concrete ways that Paul's instruction provides us with guidance in living out our motherhood "in Christ."

2

God Displays His Handiwork in the Maternal Instinct

"SHE'S EATING HER BABY!"

My daughter shrieked as we were watching a television show about animals. The narrator coolly explained that when they feel threatened, the mothers in this species of the animal kingdom eat their young.

I comforted my daughter. "Don't worry, Sweet Pea. I would never eat you. Even though your little toes look *so tasty*." More shrieking ensued as I pretended to eat her toes.

The Mother Bear

I feel like I could lift a bus to protect my offspring, but if you ask me to hand over my peanut butter banana smoothie to one of them, then I have to really think about it. A mother's instinct to nurture her child is a funny thing. I don't think I'll ever forget one particular incident when my second daughter was an infant and she got lost in a close-to-rioting crowd for 30 seconds.

We were in a crowd of a few thousand people who were barred from entering a Metro station after a fireworks show at the inauguration of the Burj Khalifa, the world's tallest building. Thousands of onlookers had arrived via the Metro to watch the fireworks show at the base of the building, so thousands of us needed to use the trains to get home. But directly after the fireworks were over, the trains weren't yet ready to be boarded because the crews were working hard behind the scenes to facilitate this massive number of commuters.

It was very late. We were exhausted and hungry, and we all wanted to go home. We stood huddled in a crowd that was growing more restless by the minute. There was no space to move, and people stood so close together that I had to lift our toddler up off the ground so she wouldn't be crushed. The baby was safe in the stroller. Then finally the armed guards opened the doors to the train station and shouted above the din of the crowd for families with babies to enter.

What a relief! At last! We could start the journey home. The guards cleared safe paths for young families to enter the station, but we were far away from the door. People were so densely packed that we couldn't move a centimeter forward. A man standing nearby noticed our family and suggested that I fold the stroller so he and his friend could lift the stroller above the crowd toward the open doors. We thought this was a great idea. Since my husband couldn't carry our baby or toddler or lift the stroller himself because of the nerve disease in his arms, I said, "Thank you!"

I unclipped baby Norah from her stroller and handed her to the woman next to me so I could fold the stroller. I just needed two seconds to get the stroller out of the way so we could try to push ourselves through the crowd. But in the second it took me to fold the stroller, my baby disappeared from my sight. The stroller went crowd surfing, and apparently so did Norah, and I felt a near-primal surge of rage cause my entire body to start trembling. My vocal chords reached a magnitude previously un-reached by my small voice as I let loose a blood-curdling scream:

"WHERE'S. MY. BABY?"

The crowd, which until this point had been alternatively mur-muring and shouting, fell silent. I think I even scared myself.

Hundreds of eyes turned in my direction as I frantically scanned the crowd for my daughter. People held their breath, and a concerned whisper started to ripple through the masses.

Even as I am typing this I am beginning to feel an aftershock of that adrenaline surge. Then within one breathless moment, we found ourselves being pushed through the crowd and into the open doors of the train station almost like osmosis.

And praise God, there was baby Norah, safe and sound, crying in the arms of a well-meaning fellow traveler. Somehow my baby had been handed from the first person to another and to another, and the last man who held her had entered the train station.

Relieved and infuriated at the same time, I snatched her away and growled, "Give me *my baby*." The "mother bear" was still livid about the whole drama. I fished out our stroller from a pile of other crowd-surfed strollers and clipped the baby back into her seatbelt, and we made our way to the elevator to catch the first train. During the entire 45 minutes home, both my husband and I wept. As the tension from this situation began to lift, all the "what ifs" swirled through our minds, and we poured out our anxieties to God and gratefully praised him for intervening on our behalf.

Christlike Motherhood

You may have felt like a mother bear at times, when protecting or defending your children, but your instinctive motherhood is indeed different from that of a brute animal's. In his very Puritan-esque language, Richard Baxter described how God created the maternal instinct to the praise of his glory:

> Women especially must expect so much suffering in a married life, that if God had not put into them a natural inclination to it, and so strong a love to their children, as maketh them patient under the most annoying troubles, the world would ere this have been at an end, through their refusal of so calamitous a life.
>
> Their sickness in breeding, their pain in bringing forth, with the danger of their lives, the tedious trouble night and day; which they have with their children in their nursing and their childhood; besides their subjection to their husbands, and continual care of family affairs; being forced to consume their lives in a multitude of low and troublesome businesses: all this, and much more would have utterly deterred that sex from marriage, if nature itself had not inclined them to it.[7]

Above and beyond the animal kingdom in which there are numerous displays of mother-bear traits, as humans we have a *redemptive* goal and purpose for our maternal instinct. When we nurture our children by faith, we are not merely going back to Eden in the likeness of Eve, the mother of all living, who clothed herself in fig leaves after she sinned. Instead of clothing ourselves in fig leaves and the filthy rags of our "good deeds" of self-righteousness, we clothe ourselves in the righteousness of Christ, taking part in God's plan to redeem creation through Jesus. Having been born again, we walk on this earth in the newness of eternal life in Christ, going about the business he has for us. This business, specifically, is discipling the nations (Matt. 28:18–20). The outcome of our work is that people will praise our Father when they see our good deeds, and God's glory will fill the earth.

The image of God is most gloriously displayed in Christ Jesus, who is the exact image of the invisible God (Col. 1:15). By God's common grace, a mother's instinct to suffer, to love, to exercise patience, to endure pain, and to work for the good of her children is a reflection of the image of God. Through the grace shown to us in the gospel, there is something distinctly Christlike about a mother's love for her child.

Sisters for Life Together

Also, through the grace shown to us in the gospel we see how Christ's love transforms our love for other mothers in Christ as well. We share one Lord and one faith, and together we're discipling our children to love Jesus. By God's grace we are to put off the old self, which instinctively prefers to lord over other mothers, and we put on the new self, which loves holiness (Eph. 4:20–24). We put away falsehood, and we speak truth to other mothers, for we are members of one another. We don't angrily sin against each other and hold grudges for the devil to use in his wicked work of causing division. We speak words to one another that are good for building up and giving grace to our hearers. We throw away all bitterness, slander, and malice that we feel toward other moms. Instead, we are kind to each other, tenderhearted, forgiving one another, as God in Christ has forgiven us (Eph. 4:25–32).

Since our hearts have been knit together in love through Christ (Col. 2:2), we share a bond that runs deeper than any brand loyalty, denomination, shared interest, or tribe (both the ethnic and ideological kinds). Sisters in Christ enjoy an abiding sweetness of fellowship as their upbringing and opinions seem so pale in comparison to the unity of their faith in Christ.

It makes sense, then, that together as God's holy and beloved chosen ones, we are to put on compassionate hearts, kindness, humility, meekness, and patience toward one another. If we find that we do not have anything nice to say about our sister in Christ, then we ought to fill our hearts with something else (Pss. 19:14; 71:8; Matt. 15:18). If we find that we have segregated ourselves into cliques, divided over petty things, or imagined ways we think we are better than one another, then we ought to remind ourselves that we are all part of one body. We know we must bear with one another and forgive each other of the complaints we have, just as God in Christ has forgiven us (Col. 3:12–13). This is all part of what it looks like to love one another with the distinguishing love that marks us as Christ followers (John 13:35). We treasure Christ when we treasure our sisters whom Jesus died to save.

These Christian virtues and ideals are quite agreeable and lovely to us. What woman doesn't want to be more compassionate? What woman doesn't need to be more patient? Yet we so often find that we would rather throw a dirty look across a room than wade through a crowd in order to humbly admonish our sister with God's wisdom. We rather like our divisions, our stature in our clique, and our zeal for influence over other women's personal choices.

We know we have a heart problem and that our affections are disordered. Christ *is* lovely to us, we *are* united to him by faith, and we *do* long to see his kingdom established here on earth. We want to possess these virtues in increasing measure so that we're effective and fruitful in our knowledge of the Lord Jesus. The idea of spiritual constipation comes to mind, and that scenario seems quite unpleasant and uncomfortable. Repentance and faith are in order.

By faith we grasp the glorious fact that we need the love of Christ to control us (2 Cor. 5:14) and give us the desire to love one another with sisterly affection and outdo one another in showing honor (Rom. 12:10). Of primary importance in our growth in godliness is that we abide in Christ and he in us (John 15:1–11). Apart from Christ we can do nothing. But as we are united to Christ by faith, the Spirit takes up residence in our souls and assures our hearts that we are daughters of God. Romans 8:1–2 says, "There is therefore now no condemnation for those who are in Christ Jesus. For the law of the Spirit of life has set you free in Christ Jesus from the law of sin and death."

Through Christ we are free from the penalty of sin and free to love others as he has loved us. This Christ-provided, Christ-empowered love has a context—the garden of community. Paul prays in Ephesians 3:17–19 "that Christ may dwell in your hearts through faith—that you, being rooted and grounded in love, may have strength to comprehend with all the saints what is the breadth and length and height and depth, and to know the love of Christ that surpasses knowledge, that you may be filled with all the fullness of God."

Being "filled with all the fullness of God" is a phrase Paul used to describe spiritual maturity. This maturity, as he describes it, is attained as we explore the unlimited dimensions of Jesus's love. Do you see how Paul has planted the context of our spiritual maturity in the garden of community? He prays that we would have strength together "with all the saints." Christ dwells in our individual hearts through faith, and his love that surpasses knowledge is experienced in community.

We need other Christian women in our lives to help us grasp how wide, how long, how high, and how deep is the love of Jesus. Compartmentalizing our spiritual life away from our interactions with other women is unhelpful and spiritually damaging. When we relegate our fellowship with other women to discussions of fleeting things and avoid talking about how eternity is pressing on our hearts, we're not doing ourselves or our friends any favors.

Christian women are sisters on the deepest level of community, bonded in Christ together for all eternity. To borrow from the knitting motif one more time, Jesus is not just a mere "common thread" that we share as sisters in Christ—he is the tapestry. Jesus is the very head we are growing up into in every way as we build ourselves up in his love (Eph. 4:15–16). It's true that other mothers can give you great advice on childcare and support your parenting decisions, but Christian sisters can give each other so much more. Jesus gives us himself, and he gives us sisters to strengthen each other as we learn more about his love that surpasses knowledge.

God designed us to need each other.

Pushing Back the Gates of Hell

Choosing to nurture and sustain life through the giving of your body, your livelihood, and your future flies in the face of our worldly society. Whenever mothers choose to give of themselves, it is evidence of God's preserving grace in our fallen world.

When Adam and Eve disobeyed God in the garden of Eden, God responded with mercy. He had instructed them not to eat from the tree of the knowledge of good and evil, "for in the day that you eat of it you shall surely die" (Gen. 2:17). But Adam and Eve didn't drop dead on the spot the moment their teeth sank into the delicious fruit.

Instead, they lived to hear these gracious words from the mouth of God. God cursed Satan, who had come to Adam and Eve in the body of the serpent in order to tempt them. God said to the serpent, "I will put enmity between you and the woman, and between your offspring and her offspring; he shall bruise your head, and you shall bruise his heel" (Gen. 3:15).

Life! If there is going to be a Savior who will bruise the head of the serpent, then that means the man and the woman will have offspring. *What mercy!*

Part of the curse that God pronounced that day in the garden involved pain in childbearing for the woman, and she would also be afflicted with a sinful desire to rule over her husband (Gen. 3:16). Man would have to fight a cursed earth for food "by the sweat of your face" (Gen. 3:17–19). Adam and Eve deserved to die right on the spot for their sin. But in his matchless grace God promised that there would be *life*.

Looking forward to God's future grace in sending a savior, by faith Adam "called his wife's name Eve, because she was the mother of all living" (Gen. 3:20). Then God slaughtered an animal and made animal-skin clothes for Adam and Eve (Gen. 3:21). And the human race was preserved by the grace of God to wait for the promised child, who would destroy God's enemy once and for all.

The demonic powers believed God's promise too. They understood that the foretold offspring of the woman would crush the head of Satan. Satan would spend the next millennia looking for the promised one in order to destroy him. "The least of these" (Matt. 25:40, 45) are image bearers of God. No wonder Satan hates them and works to snuff them out of existence and poison their innocence.

The Author of Life Sustains Our Lives

We offspring of the first man and woman all experience death as we return to the dust from which we were made. Speaking in terms of statistics, ten out of ten people die. Death is not our "friend" or a "sweet relief from life"; death is "the last enemy" that must be destroyed (1 Cor. 15:26). Death is a terror, part of the curse—a separation of our soul from our body (Gen. 2:17; 3:19, 22; Rom. 5:12; 8:10; Heb. 2:15).

Even Jesus, the one who would rise from the dead victorious over death, had no whimsical ideas about death. The author of life, who gives *bios* and *zoë*, was overcome with grief at his friend's tomb (John 11:1–44). Jesus came to take away this curse. Death is thwarted by God's mercy. "For the wages of sin is death, but the free gift of God is eternal life in Christ Jesus our Lord" (Rom. 6:23).

Through his death on the cross Jesus paid our debt to take away the terrible sting of death, and he gives us victory over our last enemy. Jesus's "instinct" compelled him to set his face toward Jerusalem, where he would allow himself to be crucified to redeem and sustain and glorify those whose hope is in him.

Jesus has saved us to the uttermost so that we do not mourn as those who have no hope (1 Thess. 4:13). We mourn the death of our loved ones knowing that God's love is more powerful than the jaws of death. Death claims the lives of believers, but death cannot hold them, as these precious ones are counterclaimed by Jesus. The saints live forever in God's presence, where they are more alive than they've ever been.

This powerful love of God's is ours not only in our deaths but also in our everyday lives. The same power that raised Jesus from the dead will raise our bodies in the resurrection. "If the Spirit of him who raised Jesus from the dead dwells in you, he who raised Christ Jesus from the dead will also give life to your mortal bodies through his Spirit who dwells in you" (Rom. 8:11). Jesus offers his power to mothers who will live in their mundane by faith as suffering, loving, patient, enduring, hard-working daughters of the King. In labor and birth, or persevering in adoption paperwork, and prayerfully pursuing our children's good, and all of the things we experience—the author of life sustains us.

The Bible says that if we share in Christ's death through our faith in his substitution for our sin, we therefore also share in his life (Rom. 6:1–12; Phil. 3:10–11). Christ's power is available to us as we have received Christ Jesus the Lord. We are to walk in him, rooted and built up in him and established in the faith, just as we were taught, abounding in thanksgiving. We take care so that no one might take us captive by philosophy and empty deceit that is not according to Christ. Many things seek to distract us or discourage us from the good work God has given. The world is brimming over with false hopes and nearsighted dreams for motherhood, but Jesus endures forever. Jesus is sufficient: "For in him the whole fullness of deity dwells bodily, and you have been filled in him, who is the head of all rule and authority" (Col. 2:9–10).

Jesus is glorified in our fellowship with one another as Christian mothers dwell together in unity.

Jesus defies the jaws of death as mothers choose to nurture human life by God's common grace.

Jesus is pushing back the gates of hell as mothers glory in God's particular grace of the cross in their mothering endeavors.

May the God who created us in his image receive all praise and glory in Christ Jesus through mothers made alive together with him.

Reflection

Mothers would do just about anything to defend their children—so much so that a mother defending her child has been likened to a bear robbed of her cubs. That protectiveness is instinctual. But God has hardwired women with a capacity to nurture that far exceeds that of a bear or any other animal, and when a woman is united to Christ, mothering is transformational.

1. How is a mother's instinct different from the instincts of the animal kingdom, and what is the redemptive goal for a mother's instinct?

2. What makes motherhood a reflection of God and the gospel (see p. 34)?

3. Abiding in Christ is essential for living out godly motherhood. What does John 15:1–11 teach us about the nature of abiding in Christ? What fruit is produced by abiding?

4. "It's true that other mothers can give you great advice on childcare and support your parenting decisions, but Christian sisters can give each other so much more" (pp. 38–39). According to Ephesians 3:17–19 and 4:15–16, what does that "so much more" consist of?

5. A section of this chapter is titled "Pushing Back the Gates of Hell" (pp. 39–40). How are the sacrifices inherent in

motherhood an opportunity to participate in this pushing back of hell?

Going Deeper

Christian mothers have a unique opportunity to encourage one another rather than compete. What specific instruction do we find in Ephesians 4:20–32 about *putting off* what divides and *putting on* what unites? We find similar language elsewhere in the New Testament. How do the following passages deepen your understanding of discipleship: Romans 8:12–13; Colossians 3:8; Hebrews 12:1; James 1:21; 1 Peter 2:1?

3

Mommy Brain

I REMEMBER WHEN our youngest child played his first practical joke. I was holding him on my hip at our church gathering as I talked with a friend. It was time for us to leave, so I instructed him, "We gotta go, Judson. Say 'bye' to Shami." "Bah bah!" he repeated as he waved his little hand in the air. Then he leaned toward my friend with his lips puckered. We were both delighted by his show of affection. Judson leaned in to plant a big, wet baby kiss on Shami. Giggling, she leaned her cheek toward him to receive the gift. But at the last second my son turned and planted that kiss squarely on *my* cheek instead. He dissolved into giggles.

I count this as Judson's first practical joke. Pranking each other is a cherished tradition in our family. You can imagine how proud I was of him in that moment. Even as an infant he was suited for our family culture of humor. And he did give Shami a kiss good-bye after all.

Children grow up so fast, don't they? Not a day goes by when I don't say this to myself or hear it from someone else. Even so, I don't always necessarily live like it is true.

Parental Amnesia

Despite the daily signposts I notice of my children's growth and development, I suffer from bouts of parental amnesia. Parental amnesia is not just when you walk into a room and forget why you're carrying the laundry basket with four dirty coffee mugs in it. That's called *normal*. Parental amnesia is when we forget about two things: tomorrow and eternity.

First, we forget that, Lord willing, our children will some-day grow up to be adults. I have a hard time imagining my five-year-old as a thirty-five-year-old or a sixty-five-year-old. Her big goal right now is waiting patiently to get to wiggle her first loose tooth. She chatters constantly about how hard she is working to learn how to read a clock. It's no wonder that sometimes I assume she'll be five forever and do five-year-old things forever.

The second thing we forget is that our children are so much more than just potential adults who will one day contribute to society. As much as I appreciate having little helpers empty the dishwasher, the fact of eternity prevents us from viewing our children from a utilitarian perspective. Our children are people made in God's image, and they have eternal souls, and this gives their lives value even if they live as adults with impaired maturity or never reach adulthood. Being a mother is wildly fun, yet because of eternity it is a serious joy at the same time.

As mothers, we can so easily become fixated on the immaturity of these little image bearers, who show people their boogers, that we neglect to treasure them as reflections of God's glory. In our noble efforts to practically raise our children to grow up to be adults, we often miss something. We miss the rising sun that signals another day of grace in which God has entrusted us with nurturing his little image bearers to love and honor him first and foremost and forever.

When the mundane looms larger than eternal life, we forget who God is, who we are, and who our children are. We tend to forget about tomorrow and eternity when our day is filled with the tyranny of the urgent. We supervise homework while diverting toddlers from swishing their arms in the toilet. We hand down verdicts in Mother's Court about whose toy it really is. We try not to forget to switch out the laundry to the dryer so we can have clean clothes to wear tomorrow. No wonder we struggle to remember what we did this morning, much less keep an eternal perspective.

When we have eternity in view, we respond to motherhood differently than if we lived just for the moment. We see that our children are marching toward a destiny. We consider that our temporary, fleeting struggles are passing away as we wait for Jesus, our blessed hope. We look forward to the day with anticipation of God's future grace, because our ordinary moments have meaning and eternal significance. We make sacrifices in our decision making and planning because we understand that we belong to God. God has called us to something vastly bigger than our happiness or that of our children.

As Paul Tripp said in his book *Forever*, "Forever tells us that our children will never exist at the center of their universe. Forever tells us that our children will not write their own stories, nor will we write their stories. Forever reminds us that our children do not belong to us; they belong to God. As parents we are God's agents, commissioned to advance his agenda."[8] Maintaining an eternal perspective keeps us grounded in God's purposes.

Raise Your Sights through God's Word

For me, parental amnesia settles like a fog in the morning hours. If I don't renew my mind through the truths in God's word, then the fog doesn't burn off and let the light of gospel hope shine in. By the end of the day I am lost in a cloud of discouragement that doesn't lift. We need the compass of eternity to direct our perspective.

It's easy to let our perspective get buried in an avalanche of cotton blends at Mount Laundry. Even so, we must make an effort to remember that our job is more than feeding, bathing, clothing, and facilitating education for our children. These tasks are meaningful in and of themselves because they're part of the stewardship God has given us. As Christian mothers God calls us to live with something we can see only with spiritual eyes—eternity.

The primary way that God stamps eternity on our eyeballs is by his word. If you hold a Bible upright and let the pages fall open, it will likely open up near the middle, pretty close to Psalm 119. Psalm 119 is the longest chapter in the Bible, and if you can read biblical Hebrew, then you'll notice it is an acrostic-type poem. Every line is dedicated to the appreciation and adoration of God's word.

Psalm 119 contains encouragement for mothers in their round-the-clock jobs. It's like a splash of cold water that could wake even the most bleary-eyed and sleep-deprived soul. In Psalm 119 you'll find specific, personal, "he must've read my journal (as if I had time for journaling)"–type application. Isn't it incredible how God speaks to us through his word?

I found these following verses from Psalm 119 to have concrete relevance as they inspired me to make some timely changes in my daily (and nightly) routine.

- I remember your name in the night, O Lord, and keep your law. (119:55)
- At midnight I rise to praise you, because of your righteous rules. (119:62)
- Oh how I love your law! It is my meditation all the day. (119:97)
- I rise before dawn and cry for help; I hope in your words. (119:147)
- My eyes are awake before the watches of the night, that I may meditate on your promise. (119:148)

I want to *hope in God* when my kids wake me up before my alarm. I want to *love God's word* all day when I'm entrenched in the mundane work around my house. I want to *meditate on God's promises* and *praise him* and *remember him* when I'm up with the baby at midnight and at 3 a.m. (and 10 p.m., 2 a.m., and 5 a.m. during growth spurts).

According to Psalm 119, there is no time of the day or night when God's word is *not* relevant to our lives. Even as we're more preoccupied with getting school lunches made and outfits chosen for family pictures, God's word can raise our gaze to the horizon of eternity.

Hope in Christ

The reality of forever reminds us to prioritize eternity in our hopes for our children. But before we extend an eternal perspective to others, we must be hoping in Christ. Too often, my hope is in my ever-changing circumstances. I say things like, "I really need the baby to take his nap this morning," which is a fine thing to say and a fine thing to look forward to. But if, come lunchtime, the nap hasn't happened, and I'm so emotionally wasted by it that it ruins my afternoon, then I've probably put more faith in that nap than in the never-changing circumstances of the gospel.

We mothers, like everyone else who struggles under the weight of sin, tend to forget the gospel, and our ignorance of the hope we have in Christ spawns rotten fruit such as identity crises and discontent. We need to remember that God is no less good to us when we find ourselves in a battle of wills with a preschooler in the checkout line at the grocery store than he was as his Son dragged a cross up a hill that Friday two thousand years ago.

God mercifully intercedes in those moments and shows me that his ways are above my ways. By God's grace I can resist the temptation to treat my children as interruptions to *my* will for my life. Instead, God enables me to treat my children as precious gifts he is using to shape me into his image according to *his* will for my life.

One morning my daughter ran back upstairs to get her purse before we left the house. By carrying an empty purse, she feels that she is ready to save any abandoned puppies or kittens she comes across. (One time she rescued a bird from drowning in our apartment's pool and carried it in her purse to the grassy lot nearby.) While I wrangled our family circus out the door, I thought about calling after her to just leave the purse behind. But something made me stop in the doorway with bags dangling off of me. I was impressed by the thought that it seemed like just yesterday that this child was a helpless baby. She needed to be cared for in every way. And now, just a heartbeat later, it seemed, she already wanted to nurture others and had the ability to do so. Someday this sweet child may have greater responsibilities to help the helpless.

In that moment I chose to enjoy God's work as this scene unfolded. I decided against telling her to just get in the car. She bounded up the stairs to fetch her purse.

In light of eternity, I want to seize day-to-day opportunities to lift my daughter's sights to admire God and image him. I need to do this myself! My train of thought was interrupted as she skipped over the bottom two steps and landed in the foyer with her purse in hand. "I got it!" she breathlessly announced. "Now I can bring home baby animals like Jesus brings home us!"

Sometimes God uses our children to remind us of the eternal perspective that we've forgotten. They grow up so fast, don't they?

Embracing Forever

Thinking well and often of eternity is not a doom-and-gloom prospect. When we deny the reality of eternity or live in ignorance of it, we're missing out on God's *joy*.

I realize that all of this talk of eternity and forever could conjure up a feeling of urgency in regard to how little time we have. To a degree, feeling the gravitational pull of finitude is healthy. Taking care of children can lend itself to being fixated on the mere minutes of the day (or night). We should pray as the psalmist did, "Teach us to number our days that we may get a heart of wisdom" (Ps. 90:12). We ought to ask the Lord to remind us that "the things that are seen are transient, but the things that are unseen are eternal" (2 Cor. 4:18).

This is why we should take caution lest we think that a mother's greatest problem is a lack of time. How tempted I am to consider a busy season as an obstacle to rejoicing in the Lord! The greatest obstruction to our joy in God is not a lack of time. When we have lost sight of an eternal perspective in our daily lives, the atonement becomes neither vital nor precious to us. A greater gift than time is the gift of forgiveness for our sins through Christ Jesus so that we can behold our holy God.

Remembering forever and living with eternity in mind are ultimately a work of God's redeeming love in our lives. I can't lay out for you a creative and strategic plan for building a heart that embraces God's purposes in eternity. None of us can muster enough willpower to love God and his glorious kingdom. Only the redeeming, all-powerful, transforming grace of God can raise our sin-besotted heart from the dead, give us eternal life, and set our gaze on Jesus, our blessed hope. Those whose soul has been revived by grace have experienced something that Jesus compared to the miracle of birth. He called it being "born again." "Truly, truly, I say to you, unless one is born again he cannot see the kingdom of God" (John 3:3).

As descendants of our first parents, whose sin in the garden brought judgment on all humanity, we stand in awe of God's common grace in ordaining that human life should continue in our fallen world. Men and women alike can see God's common grace in giving the gift of life. This is true whether or not a child comes out of your own body. This is true even if a child is taken to heaven before being born. When we consider the miracle of life, we can begin to understand what happened to us when we became born again and were given eternal life. Where there was previously not life, God gives life. What *grace*!

We are born dead in our trespasses—already at enmity with God before we spoke our first word or clung to our first prideful thought. Being separated from life in God is a living death. Through faith we see God's gift multiplied to vast numbers of people. Because Abraham believed God, we can trace our spiritual lineage back to him. "Therefore from one man, and him as good as dead, were born descendants as many as the stars of heaven and as many as the innumerable grains of sand by the seashore" (Heb. 11:12).

Abraham's faith was like Adam's. Though death reigned because of sin, they both believed God's promise of life. We can marvel at God's grace with the apostle Paul: "Much more will those who receive the abundance of grace and the free gift of righteousness reign in life through the one man Jesus Christ" (Rom. 5:17). Our best response to this good news is exultation in our merciful God. "Blessed be the God and Father of our Lord Jesus Christ! According to his great mercy, he has caused us to be born again to a living hope through the resurrection of Jesus Christ from the dead" (1 Pet. 1:3).

We walk by faith. We can tuck our children in bed by faith, close our eyes in (oft-interrupted) sleep by faith, and wake up in the morning full of faith that Jesus is our hope, even while our children grow up too fast for our liking.

———

Reflection

Are we preparing our children to be successful adults? Mothers so easily get caught on that concern, and if left unchecked, anxiety or discouragement can grow to dominate our hearts. The remedy is holding an eternal perspective, and we cultivate that through immersion in God's word.

1. *Parental amnesia* is "forgetting about two things: tomorrow and eternity" (p. 48). What are the dangers of parental amnesia, and how can we avoid them?

2. How does having an eternal perspective reshape our hopes for our children (see pp. 53–54)? In turn, how does God use our children to remind us of eternity (p. 55)?

3. "The greatest obstruction to our joy in God is not a lack of time" (p. 56). What does obstruct our joy, and how is this remedied?

4. Why is hope a vital component of a thriving faith (see Rom. 8:18–25; 1 Thess. 5:8–11; Heb. 10:19–23; 1 Pet. 1:3–9)?

5. In describing the blessings of faith, I referenced the patriarch Abraham, about whom it is written: "Therefore from one man, and him as good as dead, were born descendants as many as the stars of heaven and as many as the innumerable grains of sand by the seashore" (Heb. 11:12). Read Hebrews 11 in its entirety and note specific ways your faith is strengthened by what you see.

Going Deeper

Cultivating an eternal perspective helps us avoid parental amnesia. Read the following psalms, and for each one note how the psalmist "remembered" God and how his outlook changed as a result: Psalms 42; 63; 77; 105; 143.

4

Family Tradition #1:
We Always Need God's Grace

SELF-DISCIPLINE is a seasonal struggle for me. There are times when I'm really diligent, and there are times when diligence takes a backseat to convenience.

When my oldest child rounded the corner of preschool age, I thought that I had stumbled onto the answer to my self-discipline issues. Do you want to know the secret?

If you want to have consistent accountability for something, then just tell a preschooler what you're planning to do and make sure it contains the word "always." For example, I can't stand to see a bowl of cookie dough go into the sink to be washed unless it is already "cleaned." To combat my cookie dough self-discipline problem, I enlisted my daughter.

"Mom, you said you weren't going to eat *any more* cookie dough because you were *always* going to give the bowl to us!"

"I know I said that, Honey. But look, there's . . ."

"But we *always* lick the bowl!"

"I know you do. Here, look—the rest of the cookie dough is for you."

"You said that we always get to lick the bowl."

"I know, Mommy's sorry."

"Mom, what are you chewing?"

Preschoolers will mercilessly hold you to whatever standards you choose. They thrive on consistency. Whether it's putting on the right shoe first *always* or not mixing the Play-Doh colors *ever*, tradition is the name of the game.

So is the moral of the story to voice only the expectations that you are certain you will meet?

Leadership books discuss vision casting and shaping cultures within a corporation. Executives and managers aren't the only ones concerned with these ideas. Parents have the charge and privilege of shaping the ethos of the home. *Ethos* means, simply, "what you're all about." The word *ethos* doesn't mean much to a baby or a preschooler, but children know what they *always* do. "Daddy *always* waves goodbye to me from the driveway on his way to work." "You *always* leave my bathroom light on at night." "I *always* sit in this chair at the dinner table." "We *always* watch a movie on Friday afternoons."

I may never forget the week we lost Elmo. My daughter always took her naps with her Elmo doll in the crib. Apparently this tradition meant the world to her, because she let us know her universe was falling apart. The "we always" things are special and important. They provide the consistency our children need. The "we always" can be fun to start and continue. Some friends of ours have a tradition called Donut Saturdays, when the dad takes the kids out for donuts in the morning. What a fun tradition!

I have lots of great ideas for new traditions. One time I tried to institute a tradition called "Wordless Wednesdays": instead of arguing with each other in shrieks and shouts, we would pantomime. The kids never caught on to that one.

We Always Need God's Grace

Mothers have a strategic role in allowing the gospel to shape their homes by expecting that we are always in need of God's grace. Do you need God's grace? Or do you have what it takes to multitask your busy routine? Do you need God's grace? Or have you been "down this road before" with your husband, and your conflict will sort itself out in time? Do you need God's grace? Or do you just need Google? Do you need God's grace? Or do you pretty much have this motherhood gig in the bag?

If we want to give grace to our children, then first we must be willing to receive it ourselves from God.

In the midst of endless possibilities for the "we always" of our homes, there is one expectation that we are certain to meet every day, whether or not we are conscious of it: *we always need God's grace*. As one hymn writer wrote, "All the fitness he requireth is to feel your need of him."[9]

Grace is the most important thing for us to keep in mind as we shape the expectations of our home. Our children need to grow up knowing "We always trust God because he's willing and able to help us" and "We always praise God because he is our most valuable treasure." And we need to get up every morning knowing "I always trust God because he's willing and able to help me."

The gospel should shape the way we shape our home through our traditions. Does this mean that we ought to do catechisms with our children? Does this mean that we need to be more intentional about how we celebrate religious holidays? Perhaps. These are matters of personal preference.

The gospel, however, is not a matter of personal preference; it is news that is a matter of spiritual life and death. The gospel can shape our home as we mothers realize that we will not always meet the standards of excellence that we desire. If we want to give grace to our children, then we must be willing to receive it first from God. We tend to wallow in shame or scoff in cynicism over our inability to keep our hands out of the proverbial cookie dough. At some point, we will fail, and sometimes we will fall hard. Then we must boast in the gospel, because in it God mercifully gives us Christ to be our valued treasure. Things like "mommy guilt" cannot crush us because Christ was crushed on the cross in our stead. Jesus is our consistency; he fulfilled God's highest expectations of perfection, and in him all the promises of God find their Yes (2 Cor. 1:20). In him we find mercy in our time of need—which is *always*.

Modeling "We Always Need God's Grace"

One way to teach our children about our need for God's grace in Christ is to appropriately confess our sin to them. Ask the Lord for wisdom concerning this, and pray he would give you humility to ask forgiveness of your children when you need to do so. This is a challenge for me, as I frequently choose to minimize the offense of my sin or justify it by blaming my circumstances. It grieves me to consider how I've blamed my children's sin for my sinful response to them. We *all* always need grace.

Sometimes my children get into what I call a "sin stampede," where one child sets off another one, and then suddenly all three of them are squabbling in a frenzy. In those moments I wonder to myself, "*Why*? What would make you think that this-or-that would be the best response to her snatching your baby unicorn?"

God has been gracious to give me great clarity for the reasons for these sin stampedes: my children are sinners because they're related to me. We're all sinners who have inherited our sinful nature from our first parents, Adam and Eve. Even if I seat my children at the table to mediate the argument they are having over whose baby unicorn toy it really is, they could come out arguing over whose chair is whose.

I'm no different from my children. Dealing with annoyances and each other's sin is a part of daily life, but we can choose to respond to them in a way that honors God. I am prone to outbursts of extreme frustration. This is a big issue for me, and it says something about how I view God's sovereign goodness. It also impacts my kids.

One time the washing-machine motor burned out. This was a big deal for our big family, with lots of houseguests. Because I feel like the world revolves around me, I became very agitated by the inconvenience of a washing-machine drum that no longer agitated. I fumed from the laundry room, "Are you *kidding* me?" I may or may not have forcefully dropped the sopping wet towels onto the floor in a huff and did this exasperated scream through my gritted teeth. My kids heard my tantrum and came running. When I saw their eyes widen with fear, the Holy Spirit made me aware of my sin. My heart was at once grieved by sin and overjoyed by my Rescuer, and I repented publicly. By God's grace I took the opportunity to remind the kids (and myself) of God's mercy to save people who think the world revolves around them, when the world exists for him instead. How good is our God to use ordinary moments to sanctify us!

We always need grace. Being forgiven of our sin upon being born again in Christ Jesus by faith through grace is just the beginning. Salvation, in short, means being united to Christ. And even though we continue to sin and are tempted every day to sin, Jesus, our great high priest, stands willing and able to come to our aid. We can confidently place all our trust in Jesus—he is able! Our children will take notice when we treasure Jesus in the midst of our temptations to sin. By God's grace, our example of faith will testify that "Jesus Christ is the same yesterday and today and forever" (Heb. 13:8)—*always.*

———

Reflection

If we want to give grace to our children, then first we must be willing to receive it ourselves from God. We set high standards—for our kids, our home, and our marriage. But what happens when we fail to meet the standards we set? Let's face it: we all fail to measure up. But this is precisely where the gospel meets us in practical ways. The good news of the gospel is grace for our failures. It's God's high standards that count, not ours, and in him we have all we lack.

1. "Mothers have a strategic role in allowing the gospel to shape their homes by expecting that we are always in need of God's grace" (p. 63), and this poses a question: Do we need God's grace? We know the correct answer, but our response to daily pressures shows what we really believe. With that in mind, how would you answer?

2. What is the prerequisite for giving grace to our children (see p. 65)?

3. The gospel should shape our homes, including our family traditions. Discuss how you might incorporate this wisdom into your home and family life.

4. What are some ways you can model grace to your children? Give specific examples.

5. How does Hebrews 4:14–16 conquer "mommy guilt"?

Since then we have a great high priest who has passed through the heavens, Jesus, the Son of God, let us hold fast our confession. For we do not have a high priest who is unable to sympathize with our weaknesses, but one who in every respect has been tempted as we are, yet without sin. Let us then with confidence draw near to the throne of grace, that we may receive mercy and find grace to help in time of need.

Going Deeper

"Salvation . . . means being united to Christ" (p. 67). Meditate on the following passages that pertain to being "in Christ" and note what you discover: Romans 3:21–24; 6:11, 23; 8:1–2, 38–39; 1 Corinthians 1:28–30; 2 Corinthians 2:14; Galatians 3:26; Ephesians 2:4–10.

PART 2

————————

MOTHERHOOD
AS WORSHIP

5

A Mother's "Call to Worship"

IT'S SORT OF A JOKE around our house that if someone wants to wake up at a certain hour, all you have to do is set the alarm for ten minutes later than that specific time. The kids will beat the alarm clock every time and wake up earlier than you hope they will. A friend of mine likes to say that children are efficient alarm clocks, except they don't have snooze buttons.

When I got married my lifestyle changed. No longer single, I adapted to life with my husband, flexing and adjusting to our new life together. When I became a mother my lifestyle changed again. There were new routines to learn, adjust, readjust, and relearn. The parenting adage "every baby is different" is true, and mothers are different too, even as we learn and grow.

Me Time, Quiet Time—It's All God's Time

One of the first major changes occurred in the area of spiritual disciplines. I had been accustomed to having my own time. Right around the moment when my belly first eclipsed my feet, women started warning me, "Enjoy your time now while you can!" I knew this was true; I had watched my own mother give of her time to my sisters and me. I did not, however, imagine that the first thing to slip out of my daily schedule would be my regular devotional time with the Lord. Sadly, my initial reaction was to blame my baby and the new stage of life.

I had a skewed perspective of time, believing it was mine to organize however I pleased. *Me* time and *quiet* time kicked and screamed on their way out the door as life as a young mom burst onto the scene. My disciplined, rigorous study of God's word suddenly seemed to happen only for the papers I wrote for my professors at seminary. I realized that the only time I prayed was when I wasn't busy with the baby, and I was busy taking care of her all the time. I confessed to a friend that becoming a mother made me feel that I had forgotten the Lord, and my practice of the spiritual disciplines was revealed to be codependent on my environment.

Serenity, silence, and solitude are good things. God uses quietness to tune our hearts to listen to him through his word. Silence can help us pray without added distractions. In the peacefulness of our surroundings, the Lord can still our busy hearts. "Truly alone" time with the Lord is a gift. But so are the times when you're ringmaster-ing your family circus. The Lord is just as near to you when you're using a bulb sucker on a tiny, congested nose and as you're summoning the wisdom of Solomon to settle a spat over a disputed toy.

My spiritual life languished when my first child was born. This wasn't her fault in the least. I was under the false assumption that the Holy Spirit comforted, guided, and assured me only when my schedule was cleared out or when I had my journal sitting on my lap. I thought that I couldn't hear God if there was noise in my life.

When the noise and busyness came, I failed to make an effort to have communion with God. I got into the bad habit of calling the day a wash—spiritually speaking—if I wasn't the first person awake to enjoy the silence and solitude in our home. I would be frustrated to no end when something or someone refuted my well-laid plans to commune with the Lord in silence first thing in the morning. The Spirit made me acutely aware of the grossness of my sin, bringing to my mind passages about the Lord's kindness. In particular, this description of God's tender mercy toward sinners really softened my heart: "A bruised reed he will not break, and a faintly burning wick he will not quench" (Isa. 42:3). I knew that if I was a bruised reed or a faintly burning wick, it was only by the grace of God. I felt that I had so many things to be bitter about. The chief bitter root that had wrapped around my heart was that I had to do all the physical work of raising our baby because of my husband's physical disability. "If only I had my husband's physical help to depend on, then maybe I would have time for the Lord" was my false thinking. Little did I realize that God's kindness was about to prevail upon my embittered heart (Rom. 2:4).

I sensed that my perspective on the nature of spiritual life as a young mother was being rattled and reshaped. I had an edifying conversation with a dear friend. She shared with me 2 Corinthians 9:8: "God is able to make all grace abound to you, so that having all sufficiency in all things at all times, you may abound in every good work." God plans the end from the beginning, and he governs all the time in between, and he is able to give me the grace I need for the times he has planned right when I need it so that I can be about his will. If Jesus has assured me that he is with me to the end of the age (Matt. 28:20), then surely he is with me in all of my baby carrying, housecleaning, car driving, nighttime parenting, and husband helping.

So-Called Interruptions

When we feel that our environment must be "just so" in order to have fellowship with God, any wild-card elements inherit the name "Interruption." A toddler's plea for help with a game is an interruption. The children's early bedtime is an interruption. The baby who refuses to settle down is an interruption.

What if God wants to fellowship with us right where we are—even in the commotion of ordinary life? Most assuredly, he does. Consider how the triune God is working to ensure that you behold his glory throughout your days and nights.

Your heavenly Father is sovereign over all things. A sparrow drops its feather on the ground, escaping the clutches of a curious little boy. A car battery dies in the parking lot after a playdate at the same moment your overtired children reach their limit. A pacifier falls out of a baby's mouth just before the baby nods off to sleep. Nothing—*nothing* happens without the sovereign Lord's ordaining it. He is trustworthy and praiseworthy in every moment in every circumstance.

The eternal Son of God is *Immanuel*—God with us. Jesus fulfilled God's holy law, was crucified in our place, rose victorious from the dead, and is reigning at the Father's right hand. Jesus satisfied God's wrath against sin and purchased us from the slavery of sin. By faith we receive Jesus's perfect righteousness, and he creates in us new hearts that are prone to love him. Even when you don't feel this is true about yourself, a daughter of the King, it is. Even when you imagine that your life is hell and you have forgotten that you've been transferred into the kingdom of God's marvelous light, you're still his forever. You can be sure that nothing will separate you from God's love for you in Christ Jesus your Lord—"neither death *nor life*" (Rom. 8:38).

The Holy Spirit of God indwells the hearts of believers and writes God's law on their hearts. When we meditate on God's word, the Spirit delights to confirm in our hearts that God is who he says he is. The Spirit graciously awakens us to the affliction of our sin, and he enlivens in us an affection for God's holiness. When we put our hand to the plow (or rather, the scrub brush), the Spirit enlivens us to work as unto the Lord. The Spirit helps us in our weakness and ignorance, praying for us as we don't know what to pray for. The Holy Spirit is like the neuron that travels from our taste buds to our brains with the message that dark-chocolate-covered orange slices are exquisite. When we taste things such as providence or our union with Christ, it's the Spirit who tells our hearts that *the Lord is good*.

An Invitation to Worship God

In our church's weekly corporate worship gatherings, we have what you call "the Call to Worship." A service leader stands up in front of the congregation with the microphone and reads a portion of Scripture, inviting everyone to worship God. In line with the "so-called interruptions" idea, mothers hear "calls to worship" throughout their days and nights. If we have ears to hear these invitations, then we have opportunities to worship the Lord, who is nearer to us than we often realize.

Babies cry for food, warmth, company, and love. They plead for our help. The cries of our precious little ones remind us that we're not too different from them. We too are helpless and in a desperate estate; we desperately need the Lord. God's word instructs us not to give up crying out to him until he answers. Tune your heart to listen for times to acknowledge your neediness before the Lord. "*Incline your ear, O LORD, and answer me, for I am poor and needy*" (Ps. 86:1).

Our hearts can be called to worship even through cries of anger. Frustrated children shriek indignantly over the loss of a treasured possession from the toy box. Justice must be served! How about you? Do you ever feel righteous indignation over injustice? Do you allow yourself to feel grief over your own sin? Do you dull your conscience with

"Oh, well, what can be done?" when you see the horror of evil in our world? When a Christian acknowledges the wickedness of sin and evil, the Spirit comforts her heart and leads her in exaltation of the God who vanquishes his enemies with perfect justice. When you feel frustration and indignation well up inside you, remember what God's word says about whose prerogative it is to execute justice. Respond in your heart with a posture of peaceful repose in God's plan to conquer his enemies. "But the wicked will perish; the enemies of the LORD are like the glory of the pastures; they vanish—like smoke they vanish away" (Ps. 37:20). And reach out to those around you in mercy and love, serving as a humble servant.

"Watch me, Mommy!" Over the lilting melodies playing through the speakers, a tiny ballerina eagerly invites me to watch her twirl. She wants to share her joy with any and all who will watch and be enchanted by the music and dancing. Her expectation of shared joy reminds me of how Jesus invites me to share in his infinite joy forever. Have you ever noticed that a young child will not stop inviting you to share in her joy until you relent and do so? Jesus's joy is neither short-lived nor easily distracted; it is complete and reaches to the uttermost depths of our hearts. Respond by faith to Jesus's invitation to satisfy you fully forever. "*These things*

I have spoken to you, that my joy may be in you, and that your joy may be full" (John 15:11).

Through the recycled air of the car I can hear whining coming from the backseat. Impatience is made manifest in complaining. This is so like me. I want what I want, and I want it yesterday. As I toss a bag of crackers into the hands of a preschooler who's got the munchies, I'm reminded of how it's hard to complain when your heart is filled with praise. You've heard the admonition "Don't talk with your mouth full." But the Bible says otherwise—we are to talk with our hearts and mouths full! "My mouth is filled with your praise, and with your glory all the day" (Ps. 71:8); "Praise the LORD! I will give thanks to the LORD with my whole heart, in the company of the upright, in the congregation" (Ps. 111:1); "The good person out of the good treasure of his heart produces good, and the evil person out of his evil treasure produces evil, for out of the abundance of the heart his mouth speaks" (Luke 6:45). For me, the call to worship that I have the hardest time hearing is the one in the early morning. For the years our young family had to share a bedroom, I was regularly wakened by excited, breathless whispers in my ear, announcing the forthcoming sunrise. My groggy disbelief is but a fraction of the weariness and soul heaviness that was felt by the women who arrived at a certain tomb before dawn and were not expecting to behold the risen Son.

But because Jesus did rise from the dead, every glorious sunrise (even the early ones) marches forward and points us to look ahead to the day that is coming, which will be the end of darkness forever. On that day we will all see our Savior face-to-face with no more doubting or lukewarm affections or soul sluggishness. Then we will call each other to worship God forever and ever, saying, "*To him who sits on the throne and to the Lamb be blessing and honor and glory and might forever and ever!*" (Rev. 5:13).

How a Baby's Cry Silences Satan

When a baby cries out in the middle of the night—hungry, cold, lonely, wet, uncomfortable—we mothers often feel inconvenienced. *Again? What now?* We sigh deeply, groan, mutter, rub our eyes, and reluctantly shift our tired legs off the bed and onto the floor once again.

But those tears—bleating, frustrated, desperate, and everything in between—are announcing so much more than what your baby wants or needs. They are cries that silence the enemy, who hates God, hates God's creation, and hates the gift of life itself. Your helpless baby's tears are tearing the tauntings of the devil asunder.

The stage for the baby's broadcast is cosmic (and I'm not just talking about the ear-piercing volume). In Psalm 8:1 we read, "O Lᴏʀᴅ, our Lord, how majestic is your name in all the earth! You have set your glory above the heavens." The Lord's name, that is, his reputation—everything about who he is and what he is about—is exalted above everything and everyone who would challenge him.

Verse 2 continues this thought and compels us to feel a sense of awe at the strength of our Lord. He magnifies his strength through weakness. "Out of the mouth of babies and infants, you have established strength because of your foes, to still the enemy and the avenger." God's enemy is Satan, and Satan wreaks his acrid vengeance through the taking, stifling, suffocating, and maiming of life.

Consider, as King David did in Psalm 8, the majesty of God in creating the cosmos: "When I look at your heavens, the work of your fingers, the moon and the stars, which you have set in place, what is man that you are mindful of him, and the son of man that you care for him?" (8:3–4). The created universe is an understatement when compared to the glory of its Creator. There's nothing more breathtaking than the heavens—except God himself. The heavens he created are merely a reflection of his glory. Our Milky Way galaxy alone is home to at least two hundred billion stars. What wonder must we feel in our heart when we consider the magnitude of God's infinite glory.

That little baby bears the image of the Holy One. On the cosmic stage of God's glory displayed in the universe, the infant's cries silence the insolent boasts of God's enemy. God ordained that life would continue despite the devil's decrepit handmaiden, death. God granted that eternal life prevail through his Son, who rose victorious from the grave, never to see decay. God gives this eternal life away as a gift to those who would trust in his Son. Life is here to stay forever.

When you hear your baby's cries, pray for spiritually attuned "ears to hear." Listen as the Spirit summons your heart in a call to worship the sovereign Lord. He uses the weak things to shame the strong (1 Cor. 1:27); what a profoundly mysterious glimpse of the character of our God, whose purposes cannot be thwarted, interrupted, or inconvenienced.

As you're listening, watch. As your preschooler cries for his beloved plastic blue spoon ("No, Mom, not the *yellow* one!") or you hear the beginnings of a long night via the static of the baby monitor, look through these windows of grace with the eyes of your heart. See evidence of God's grace to give and sustain life in our fallen world. Believe God is with you in your good work of mothering. I know this is difficult and often painful work. But since "the sufferings of this present time are not worth comparing with the glory that is to be revealed to us" (Rom. 8:18), then let's not fix our eyes on these temporary pains but on Christ. Respond to God's calls to worship throughout your days and nights, serving and nurturing helpless little ones and worshiping the author of life.

———

Reflection

Time alone for spiritual refreshment—what Christian mother doesn't yearn for more of that? Sometimes we fear that spiritual growth must go on hold until the next season of life. But God is so much bigger than that! He is always at work in our lives—even when it seems that all is chaos.

1. Finding solitude to commune with God is a challenge for mothers. How does 2 Corinthians 9:8 help (see p. 76)?

2. Repeated interruptions throughout the day can wear us down. Before we know it, we're irritable, frustrated, and snapping at the kids. Realizing two truths helps us know peace rather than frustration: God's sovereignty and Jesus's name "Immanuel," which means "God with us." How do these truths equip us to roll peacefully with the punches?

3. How can everyday ordeals serve as "calls to worship"? There are some examples on pages 79–82. Recall some recent instances from your own life that could have been worship opportunities.

4. Jesus promises that fullness of joy is available for all his daughters. Do you believe this can be true for you, even in the midst of mothering chaos? Consider your response to Jesus's invitation in John 15:11: "These things I have spoken to you, that my joy may be in you, and that your joy may be full." How would you summarize the "these things" Jesus spoke of (see 15:1–10)?

5. God magnifies his strength through weakness (see Ps. 8:2 and 1 Cor. 1:27). How does this knowledge help us respond with grace to chronic inconveniences?

Going Deeper

Time is precious, and we can so easily panic when our hours get swallowed up in activities that seem trivial and unending. How does Psalm 139 alter your thinking not only about your time but also about those activities that seem so trivial?

6

A Mother's Love

"I LOVE YOU THIS MUCH!"

Since they first learned to speak, our children have been catechized with this question and answer most evenings before bedtime: "Mommy and Daddy love you. But who loves you most of all?"[10] This question is answered with a resounding "Jesus!" by all the tiny voices in the room.

The psalmist entreats the Lord for this kind of love: "Show us your steadfast love, O LORD, and grant us your salvation" (Ps. 85:7).

Jesus announces that he is the answer to the cry of the psalmist's heart: "Greater love has no one than this, that someone lay down his life for his friends" (John 15:13). Paul describes Jesus's sacrificial love in Romans 5:7–8: "For one will scarcely die for a righteous person—though perhaps for a good person one would dare even to die—but God shows his love for us in that while we were still sinners, Christ died for us." A few verses earlier in Romans 5:5, we learn about the comforting ministry of the Holy Spirit, who pours out the love of God into our heart.

A Mother Loves Because God First Loved Her

Indeed, the steadfast love of the Lord is better than life (Ps. 63:3) because his love gives us *his* life. Because of his love we are able to love. "We love because he first loved us" (1 John 4:19).

It is this love—the love of Christ—that compels Christian mothers to love their children. The love of Christ in her heart is what overflows when a mother speaks kindly to her children even when they don't speak kindly back. The love of Christ echoing in her soul is what causes a mother to extend grace to her children, who can hear a bag of chips opening from across the apartment but fail to hear certain words spoken in their presence, like "Clean. Your. Room." The love of Christ controls us as we speak the words of the gospel of hope to our children time and again. The love of Christ convinces mothers not to live for themselves but to live for him, who for their sake died and was raised (2 Cor. 5:15).

A mother who has faith in Christ Jesus loves because of the hope laid up for her in heaven (Col. 1:4–5). We know this is true because the Bible says it is true. Personally, another reason that I know this is true is that my own mother sacrificially, unconditionally loved me because of her faith in Christ. Faith in future grace is undoubtedly what sustained my mother's heart through my self-induced nightmare adolescence. I was a scoffer; she loved me sincerely. I walked in the counsel of the wicked; she loved me enough to tell me that I was going astray. I stood in the way of sinners; she loved me enough to tell me about Jesus's forgiveness. No mother's nightmarish valley is so dark that Jesus cannot bear her burdens the whole way through.

Hope in God's future grace through Christ Jesus is what binds a mother's heart together when all she feels like doing is falling apart into a million pieces. We know that because of the Lord's great love, we are not consumed, and his compassions never fail (Lam. 3:22). Even Jeremiah, who saw the desolation of his beloved city, set his hope on the Lord God himself and not on his circumstances. He recognized that God's mercies are new every morning (Lam. 3:23). And this faith in God's future grace is what enabled Jeremiah to say, " 'The Lord is my portion,' says my soul, 'therefore I will hope in him' " (Lam. 3:24). Don't you love how Scripture makes your heart stagger under a weight of glory while holding you steady at the same time? Imagine—the Lord is your portion. Not convinced? Just look at what the Father did to his only Son (who willingly gave himself on your behalf) in order that Jesus could make you his treasure and you could make him yours.

I'm tempted to throw all of my eggs in the basket of behavior modification, cross my fingers, and hope for the best. But salvation for moms and their children belongs to the Lord. We—all of us—must place our trust in the Son, clinging to his cross, and rejoice in the hope of the glory of God.

Love Is Complicating

A mother's Spirit-empowered sacrificial love is what enables her to willingly complicate her life for the sake of her children. Just think of the extraordinary complications you've observed in your own life, your mother's life, and in the lives of other mothers you know. The many adoptive mothers I know, in particular, have willingly and cheerfully complicated their lives in order to sacrificially love their children.

Christlike love willingly and cheerfully makes room for complications in order to look to the interests of others. If we have received encouragement, comfort, affection, and sympathy from Christ and have been grafted into him by his

Spirit, then we should overflow with that same encourage-ment, comfort, affection, and sympathy that flows from unity with Christ (Phil. 2:1–2). As we serve our family, we take care to avoid serving them in such a way as to bloat our egos; in humility we count others more significant than ourselves (Phil. 2:3). When it comes to raising our children, there is no task too humiliating when we have this mindset—the mindset of Christ Jesus the humble servant.

Consider how the Lord Jesus Christ willingly and cheerfully complicated his life so that he could share his life with us. Al-though he was in the form of God, he "did not count equality with God a thing to be grasped, but emptied himself, by taking the form of a servant, being born in the likeness of men. And being found in human form, he humbled himself by becoming obedient to the point of death, even death on a cross" (Phil. 2:6–8). As if becoming God incarnate wasn't humbling enough for the Creator, this innocent author of life further humbled himself by allowing himself to be crucified like a criminal.

It's true that our children need to hear this life-giving gospel time and again. We mothers need to hear it too.

I remember how my attachment to "me first" became ob-vious to my whole family one balmy morning in the desert. Dave's arm surgeries have brought with them some pretty intense recovery periods and lingering physical pain. At times he cannot bathe, clothe, or feed himself. Sometimes I have had to line up my younger children next to my husband and feed them all in turns!

During one particularly difficult morning, everyone was clamoring for Mommy's help and attention. There were two wet diapers to change, nobody had clothes ready for the day, and my husband needed my help turning on the shower and the sink in the bathroom. In the din of toddler squawks, Dave had the humor to joke, "All right, kids! Whichever one of us cries the loudest has Mommy's help getting dressed first!" I did not laugh. I couldn't.

For some reason the bitterness I felt regarding my situation just ran too deep for it to be funny. I was angry, and I suppose I had been angry for a while. I had long forgotten that God is not apathetic to my situation. I had ceased to view life as a battle for joy in the midst of sorrow in a fallen world. In that moment I just wanted everyone to leave me alone. I said as much out loud through gritted teeth: "Would you all just leave me alone, please?" The children ignored me and kept whining. My husband left the bathroom in silence, leaving his morning routine unfinished.

Why was I so depleted in love for others? Why was my attitude so hostile toward the people I love the most? In my prayerful reflections on that incident, the Lord graciously revealed to me that I had a deep craving to satisfy my own needs before the needs of others. I saw how my nearly unceasing service toward my family had actually been powered by attempts to resuscitate myself through sheer willpower and control my environment. I was of the mindset that if I could just make it through another day, then I could fall asleep again and no one would bother me until the morning (maybe). I was under the impression that if I could just figure out the perfect chore chart, then the apartment would get sorted out. I thought that if I could just find the best parenting tricks out there, then the children would shepherd themselves via autopilot. And, of course, I felt that if my husband's disability would finally just go away, then we could all get on with our lives. I had forgotten the Lord, and this kind of amnesia can cast a long shadow over the soul.

Loving like Jesus loved is a dying to self a thousand deaths a day. There are times when we are not motivated by the love of Christ, and we fume at our children not because they break God's law but because they break ours. We might escalate petty wrongdoings and pointless arguments with our children. We might neglect the physical, emotional, and spiritual well-being of our children. We might take up our lives one thousand times a day (and night) and resist laying them down to serve others.

We might even serve others very well, yet all the while groaning that our children and husband aren't applauding loudly enough to congratulate our efforts.

Jesus's humility redefines our worldly ideas of what it means to serve others. He gave us a *new* commandment: "A new commandment I give to you, that you love one another: just as I have loved you, you also are to love one another" (John 13:34). We need to be redeemed and refined by God's grace. We need to submit to the Savior, who can break our bondage to serving and worshiping ourselves. When a mother takes hold of the atoning death of Christ by faith, she sees the death of her sin in the death of Christ. "There is therefore now no condemnation for those who are in Christ Jesus. For the law of the Spirit of life has set you free in Christ Jesus from the law of sin and death" (Rom. 8:1–2).

A mother whose sin has been buried with Christ in his death has been raised to new life in his resurrection. She is now a slave to righteousness (Rom. 6:18). She has a new theme song to sing—a refrain that will echo throughout her days and nights—a song of redeeming love.

Never Make Sacrifices

One of my missionary heroes is David Livingstone, a man who spent the better part of his life persevering through extraordinary hardship for the sake of the gospel in Africa. I often recall his example of endurance and faith when I'm in "I guess it could always be worse" scenarios. But that's not why Livingstone encourages me so much. Ironclad faith is not forged by considering how much more pleasant my earthly circumstances are than someone else's. "It could always be worse" cannot sustain my fragile heart. Only hope in God's enduring faithfulness is a shatterproof assurance. My heart is strengthened by considering that we have the same heavenly Father, are saved by the same Jesus, are indwelled by the same Holy Spirit, and rejoice in the same gospel. If God sustained this fellow saint, then he can carry me too.

So what does this anecdote about a missionary to Africa have to do with motherhood and sacrifices? Livingstone gave a speech at Cambridge University, which has shaped how I think about motherhood. He wasn't talking about motherhood specifically; he was speaking on having an eternal perspective and on his role as a missionary. When I read his words, I can't help but think about how the same principles are at work in my life as a mother whose hope is in the gospel. Livingstone said:

> For my own part, I have never ceased to rejoice that God has appointed me to such an office. People talk of the

sacrifice I have made in spending so much of my life in Africa. Is that a sacrifice which brings its own blest reward in healthful activity, the consciousness of doing good, peace of mind, and a bright hope of a glorious destiny hereafter? Away with the word in such a view, and with such a thought! It is emphatically no sacrifice. Say rather it is a privilege. Anxiety, sickness, suffering, or danger, now and then, with a foregoing of the common conveniences and charities of this life, may make us pause, and cause the spirit to waver, and the soul to sink; but let this only be for a moment. All these are nothing when compared with the glory which shall be revealed in and for us. *I never made a sacrifice.*

To be sure, mothers do make sacrifices for their children in a thousand little ways each day. But we have to define and evaluate these things with an eternal perspective. Like Livingstone we should ask: Is that service to my child a sacrifice that brings its own blest reward in their well-being, the consciousness of serving God, peace of mind, and a bright hope of a glorious destiny? Conversely stated, when a mother triumphs in the gospel, her bright hope in Jesus outshines *any* earthly gain she could have had from holding back from her child Jesus's sacrificial love.

So when we consider the calling, the work, and the sacrifices of motherhood in this light, with a thrill in our heart we can say that we have never made a sacrifice.

Loving Your Kids to the Glory of God Alone

It is also possible that deeds done in the name of love for a child can be exhibitions of how our hearts are like idol factories. I shudder to think of how often I justify my self-worship under the guise of "because I love my children" and exalt myself or my children to the position of God. I make much of my children and child-raising preferences, and I make little of God. This remains a huge temptation for me as I fall into this ego trap all the time, and that's why I am so thankful for how the gospel frees me from seeking my glory in parenting or in my kids. My children, although they probably can't articulate it yet, are relieved that when I treasure Jesus, they are freed from the burden of being the center of my world. No child should have to shoulder the weight of her mother's glory and reputation.

Every mother can be freed from seeking her own glory as she loves her children for the sake of Jesus's name being made famous among the nations. Perhaps the most pertinent correction I've received in light of this temptation is what Jesus told Paul about boasting: "He said to me, 'My grace is sufficient for you, for my power is made perfect in weakness.' Therefore I will boast all the more gladly of my weaknesses, so that the power of Christ may rest upon me" (2 Cor. 12:9). Do I want the power of Christ to rest on me as I mother my children? Yes, please! Then I need Jesus to free me from my craving to be worshiped for my mothering. I need to own up to my weaknesses so that I can prize Christ's power.

God's sovereign grace releases me from the worry that I'm doing a haphazard job of orchestrating my children's lives for them. The gospel reminds me that a mother's plans are not ultimate; God's are. God is the one who has created these children, and he has far more intentional intentions to glorify himself through these kids than I could ever dream up. God made these children for himself—for his name's sake.

Every mitochondrion in their little bodies exists for God's glory. The Lord knew our children's destiny before the sperm ever met the egg. He commands their destiny from before the foundations of the world. He knows the number of their days and no part of their story surprises him. He is the God to whom we want to actively, daily entrust our children. The sovereign Lord of the universe deserves our faith-filled acknowledgment of his ownership of our kids. We all belong to our Creator. When we think our children exist to serve our egos, we get distracted from our primary purpose of serving our children by teaching them who God is and how they exist to enjoy him.

Treasuring Christ as preeminent in our lives gives our children a self-sacrificing, neighbor-serving, sin-forgiving, grace-extending illustration of how God is worthy to be seen, admired, and displayed as the greatest hope we could ever have. Jesus is the one who loves us most of all with his redeeming love.

———

Reflection

Remember, "No mother's nightmarish valley is so dark that Jesus cannot bear her burdens the whole way through." It is the love of Christ that gives us hope. It's his love that enables us to persevere. And because of his love for us—and through that love—mothers can love and raise their children to the glory of God.

1. When it comes to training our kids, we tend to default to behavior modification before leaning on Christ. Why do you think this is? How does placing our trust in Christ work to alter our default?

2. Because every waking hour of a mother's life is about serving others, motherhood is a humble calling. In Philippians 2, the apostle Paul points to Christ as our example of humble service. Read Philippians 2:3–11. How does this passage alter your perspective on mothering?

3. There are times when we fume at our children not because they break God's law but because they break ours. What underlies our cravings to control (see pp. 93–94)?

4. It is easy to be tempted to make idols of our children (p. 97). In what ways do you tend to idolize your kids or your child-raising techniques? How can moms be freed from seeking the self-glory that underlies the idols of motherhood?

5. Why is weakness a key component of mothering to the glory of God (see 2 Cor. 12:2–10)?

Going Deeper

My view of motherhood has been shaped in part by reading about the life of missionary David Livingstone, and I have found encouragement in the words of a speech he delivered at Cambridge University in 1857. If you google "David Livingstone," you'll find his speech in its entirety, as well as other resources pertaining to his life. Peruse some of these resources and see how they impact your own view of motherhood.

7

Mommy Doesn't Always Know Best

EVEN IF MOM'S NOT CHOOSY, she has to choose.

At bedtime one night my oldest child approached me with a plan for tomorrow's menu: "Mom, I've got a great idea. How about tomorrow for breakfast we eat cereal. Then for lunch we eat peanut butter and jelly sandwiches with chips. Then for dinner we'll eat that leftover soup you made from today."

This sounded like a delightful plan to me so I said, "How about that. That sounds wonderful."

She added a tip: "And, Mom, you might want to write this all down. Maybe I could draw pictures next to each thing. Then you won't forget that we talked about this, and you don't have to think about it tomorrow."

My child knows me all too well. Menu planning and grocery shopping are a domestic handicap for me, so I really appreciate her input.

It seemed like I had just figured out how to cook for two when our first child came along. Then when I felt like I had sorted out how to manage meals for our little family, we moved overseas. I switched from ounces to grams, dollars to dirhams, zucchini to marrow, granola to muesli, ground beef to mince, and so on. In the first year we lived here, the grocery store made me dizzy (and often upset) with all the foreign ways of shopping and the new foods that weren't marked with nutrition labels.

Decisions about how to feed our family suddenly became complex and perplexing. There was so much I had to learn that it was overwhelming.

The Burden of Decisions

I think a lot of us feel overwhelmed when we become mothers. We feel burdened by decisions before the baby even arrives. Which prenatal vitamin should I take? How do I choose an obstetrician or a midwife? What is the best route for domestic adoption? Do we want to find out the sex of the baby? Are we open to transracial or international adoptions? Should I quit my job? When should I quit my job? How are we going to agree on the baby's name?

If you embarked on this journey unaware of all this, then the decision-making aspect of motherhood probably hit you like a ton of Play-Doh. Maybe you were shocked by how your personal choices seemed to label you as a "_____-mommy." You might have been surprised to discover values that you weren't aware you held. You no doubt have been saddened at being confronted by critics you didn't know you would have. And it is to be hoped that you have been delighted to share common ground with new friends.

There is certainly no lack of decisions a mother might make in the course of a day. Our choices range from temporal to long term. Where can a mother find wisdom? The most important decision a mother can make each day is to fear the Lord and seek his wisdom. James 1:5 says, "If any of you lacks wisdom, let him ask God, who gives generously to all without reproach, and it will be given him." This wisdom from the Lord is not a trivial pursuit of Bible Verse Roulette in which you flip through the pages of God's word until your eyes land on something that seems good to you. God's wisdom is gained by asking him for it, and his wisdom is demonstrated most profoundly in the gift of his Son. The cross of Jesus Christ is the wisdom of God that confounds the wisdom of the age. There is no deeper or more relevant wisdom that one could share than to fear the Lord and worship the God-man Jesus Christ.

The tyranny of the urgent decisions is deluding. We often feel that the most important decision we need to make in a day is about our child's extracurricular activity or whether to introduce the baby to a pacifier. Yet what impacts our daily lives much more is whether we are seeking the Lord in his word and through prayer so that he might fill us with the knowledge of his will in all spiritual wisdom and understanding. More relevant than our mothering choices or strategies is whether we are walking in a manner worthy of him, fully pleasing to him, bearing fruit in every good work and increasing in the knowledge of God (Col. 1:9–10).

We All Lack Wisdom

When I was a new mother, an older friend gave me some good advice: "Just when you figure out one stage, another stage starts. So don't get too obsessed over the details." I think what she said was quite helpful, especially to someone like me who feels a little uncomfortable with the unknowns of motherhood.

Beyond the wisdom that we lack because of our inexperience, we have a deeper problem. Our sin induces us to labor for independence from God. We don't desire his wisdom. Paul says in Romans 7:18, "For I know that nothing good dwells in me, that is, in my flesh. For I have the desire to do what is right, but not the ability to carry it out." Even when we know we need to seek God's wisdom, we have to fight against our flesh, which rails against the goodness of God. We're organic sinners; apart from Christ we're holiness intolerant.

Puritan Thomas Watson said, "Until sin be bitter, Christ will not be sweet."[11] I think Scottish minister Thomas Chalmers, who preached on "the expulsive power of a new affection," would have added: Until Christ be sweet, sin will not be bitter.

Our misplaced affection for sin needs to be evicted from the throne in our hearts by a superior power. We each need a new heart. Our holy affections need to be facilitated by the indwelling Holy Spirit, who inclines our hearts to love Jesus and be attracted to his holiness. Nothing less will do. "I know of no other way to triumph over sin long-term than to gain a distaste for it because of a superior satisfaction in God."[12]

We can't just displace our flesh and our love for the world by cataloguing all the ways we've been disappointed by our sin or by the world. Perhaps you've seen already how ineffective it is to complain to your friends about any disappointments you've had in your motherhood. Simply airing these discouragements does not provoke in us a thrilling sense of hope in God. Plummeting headlong into disenfranchisement with God's gifts is an incomplete and ultimately useless cure for the heart's ills. This kind of ascetic fervor in renouncing the beauties of motherhood is no more distinctly

Christian than the hedonism of a mother who idolizes her motherhood.

The depth of our depravity and our heart's inclination to justify itself mean something significant. They mean that merely lamenting the insufficiency of the world is an incompetent way to rescue and recover our captive hearts from wrong affections. Our hearts need to be redeemed by Jesus and made new.

The superior power of affection and devotion to Jesus can do what no lament of the world or of the temporality of God's earthly gifts could ever do. Simply telling yourself that those wrong affections will fail you is not enough. You have to introduce a greater affection to the soul—one that is "powerful enough to dispossess the first of its influence."[13]

This greater affection must have the ability to satisfy the heart like nothing else. It's like when you've tasted New York–style cheesecake made from scratch, no powdered cheesecake mix from a box will ever do. This greater affection is what renders all idols and temptations as pathetic and ridiculous and trivial by comparison.

How Do We Love Wisdom?

When babies transition into eating solid foods, we take great care in feeding them nutritious foods that are age appropriate. We mind the texture, temperature, and quantities for them because babies don't know how to do this for themselves.

How are you feeding yourself spiritually? Are you starved for God's wisdom? Do you crave God's word above all the tidbits of information, news, and status updates that are available to you? Every day we face the temptation of "how-to-ing" ourselves to death. In and of themselves, the practical tips, guides, and websites marketed to moms are very helpful. We need practical help. I just checked the search history in my web browser, and in the past 48 hours I've searched for the answers to seven practical "how-to" questions.

But making an effort to learn practical things for living is not my problem. My biggest problem is that I live under the illusion that I can do anything I put my mind to while I give lip service to needing God's wisdom. I need to know at the heart level that I cannot do anything gracefully to God's glory without the guidance and help of the Holy Spirit. Biblical doctrine, in this regard, undergirds my heart with God's truth and gives me the wisdom I need to understand that my biggest problem is not multitasking or lack of experience in mothering or domestic life. Mothers who feed their soul with the word of God will thrive as their hearts are taught by God's wisdom.

Checklists are great tools, but they have their place sub-servient to God's wisdom. We tend to prefer lists of things to do when it comes to difficult matters about which we must make decisions. "Just tell me what to do!" I hear often when counseling women who feel like they're stuck between a rock and a hard place. Theology has so much to contribute to the mother who makes decisions—difficult ones or easy ones. Theology is where practicality begins. Look at Scripture!

The fear of the LORD is the beginning of wisdom,
    and the knowledge of the Holy One is insight.
        (Prov. 9:10)

And he said to man,
"Behold, the fear of the LORD, that is wisdom,
    and to turn away from evil is understanding."
        (Job 28:28)

The fear of the LORD is the beginning of wisdom;
    all those who practice it have a good understanding.
    His praise endures forever! (Ps. 111:10)

The fear of the LORD is instruction in wisdom,
    and humility comes before honor. (Prov. 15:33)

I write with the authority of a woman who has tasted a lot of soul junk food and suffered from painful spiritual cavities. Spiritual counsel that has "empty calories" or is devoid of rich, biblical doctrine cannot and will not satisfy a soul that was made to be satisfied only with an infinite God. "Taste and see that the LORD is good! Blessed is the man who takes refuge in him!" (Ps. 34:8). We need to humbly rend our heart before we rend our internet search engines searching for answers. Psalm 34:18 says, "The LORD is near to the brokenhearted and saves the crushed in spirit." God, our wise Father, freely gives wisdom to any of his children who would ask him for it (James 1:5). He gives us his wisdom and satisfies us with himself in order to save us from wandering the desert and dying of spiritual dehydration.

Jesus is the wisdom from God. His cross is the most profound utterance of wisdom that the Holy One ever made. The atoning work of the Lamb of God confounds the wisdom of our age. By the means of his death on the cross, Jesus leads us straight to our Father through himself—the one mediator between God and man. Jesus offers us himself and his wisdom freely:

Come, everyone who thirsts,
   come to the waters;

and he who has no money,
>   come, buy and eat!
Come, buy wine and milk
>   without money and without price.
Why do you spend your money for that which is not bread,
>   and your labor for that which does not satisfy?
Listen diligently to me, and eat what is good,
>   and delight yourselves in rich food.
Incline your ear, and come to me;
>   hear, that your soul may live. (Isa. 55:1–3)

Following Christ, loving Christ, and obeying Christ are undoubtedly the most important decisions any mother could ever make. And the follow-through of these decisions comes into play each and every day.

———

Reflection

Theology is where practicality begins. But faced with countless decisions and problems to solve, we kick into crisis-control mode and simply check things off the to-do list. Yet no matter how skilled we are at problem solving, we get up and repeat the pattern the very next day. More than how-to's and checklists, our greatest need is to shift our focus upward and develop the sort of wisdom that comes only from depending on God.

1. Mothers can feel burdened by the sheer volume of decisions that must be made on a daily basis, but the primary decision of each day is to fear the Lord. What does it mean to "fear the Lord"? Develop your answer from Job 28:28; Psalm 111:10; and Proverbs 1:1–7; 8:13; 9:10–11. To what does the fear of the Lord lead?

2. Why do we all lack wisdom (see pp. 106–7)? Where in your life do you find yourself relating to the words of the apostle Paul in Romans 7:18: "For I know that nothing good dwells in me, that is, in my flesh. For I have the desire to do what is right, but not the ability to carry it out"?

3. "Until Christ be sweet, sin will not be bitter." How does that sense of sweetness come about in our hearts (see pp. 107–8)?

4. "Spiritual counsel that has 'empty calories' or is devoid of rich, biblical doctrine cannot and will not satisfy a soul that was made to be satisfied only with an infinite God." Can you identify any spiritual "junk food" that you've

partaken of recently? How do we distinguish between that and spiritually nutritious counsel?

5. What do we see about Jesus in the following passages that supplies what we so often seek in ourselves or in what this world offers: Isaiah 55:1–3; Matthew 11:28–29; and 1 Corinthians 1:20–31?

Going Deeper

Do you crave God's word? To cultivate a deeper love for Scripture, prayerfully read through Psalm 119, an acrostic poem about Scripture. What do you find in this psalm that makes you want more of God's word? Take special note of the verses that reference "wholeheartedness."

8

The Good News and Mommy's No-Good, Very Bad Day

NOT EVERY DAY, but some days, naptime can't come fast enough, because the one having the afternoon meltdown is Mommy. I remember one day when the older children were going through a whining/agitating cycle on repeat, and I asked aloud, "When is it Mommy's turn to be upset?" One child actually paused and thoughtfully replied, "Okay, Mommy. You can have a turn. That's only fair."

Even moms who haven't thrown a tantrum in a while can relate to feeling that they've had enough as they limp to the end of the day, emotionally drained and exasperated. For many of us, the frustration stems from the unreasonable expectations we have for ourselves. Instead of the sweet relief and satisfaction that come from a long day of good, hard work, we stew over the mistakes, missed opportunities, and foibles. "There are no perfect moms," we quip, but we'll die trying to prove we might be the exception.

Other moms are overwhelmed by the logistics of life itself. This is a frustration that I found myself drowning in while we transitioned overseas, hit a rough patch during my second pregnancy, and saw my husband's physical disability getting much worse. Life itself seemed impossible, much less a life overflowing with joy. It was during that time that I became convinced that cliché encouragements about life are like cheap diapers. Only the gospel can preserve your faith through a spiritual blowout. Too often we settle for throwing cliché glow sticks into the darkness of our doubts. And their light and comfort quickly fade.

Perhaps the scariest feelings in the midst of these frustrations come from one particular dark thought. It's a lie that we're tempted to believe. This idea has more to do with karma than with grace: we suspect that however the day went is how God feels about us.

Just Cut Yourself Some Slack?

What is our hope when a deluge of domestic frustrations threatens to sweep us away into the sea of despondency? Is it merely that this is just a season that will pass?

Maybe you're the frustrated mom, or you're the mom who is reaching out to encourage other desperate housewives. The daily lives of mothers around the world are different, but our hope is the same. All of us need to experience the concrete reality of a hope that is for every season and will never pass. Frustrated moms and desperate housewives have a problem that runs far deeper than our need for a break from the daily grind, though physical rest is a daily necessity.

Denying that we have no-good, very bad days only works until the next no-good, very bad day comes around. Just cutting ourselves some slack on occasion isn't going to cut it in the long run.

What we all need is to be rescued from our sin by the Son, who was cut off from the Father when he took our sin upon himself so that we could be bound to God by his grace forever. What we need to see is the light of the knowledge of the glory of God in the face of Jesus Christ shining into our hearts (2 Cor. 4:6).

Only the blazing light of the gospel can dispel our dark doubts and illumine the sin we need to repent of. Through the light of the gospel we see how God's kindness leads us to repentance. And, by his grace, God forces our frustrating circumstances to bow to his gospel purposes in our lives. God uses these situations to grow us in Christlikeness, get us sick of our sin, and teach our hearts to yearn for future grace. I love what Ed Welch said about hoping in God's future grace: "Your future includes manna. It will come. There is no sense devising future scenarios now because God will do more than you anticipate. When you understand God's plan to give future grace, you have access to what is arguably God's most potent salve against worry and fear."[14]

As we go about our work in the home, we need to see with the eyes of our heart that Christ is the righteousness to everyone who believes (Rom. 10:4). That means we don't try to launder or mend the rags of our self-righteousness as though they commend us to God. Jesus is our commendation. We don't polish our trophies of domestic accomplishment as though they give us confidence before God's throne. Christ is our confidence. It is as Jerry Bridges has said in his book *The Discipline of Grace*: "Your worst days are never so bad that you are beyond the reach of God's grace. And your best days are never so good that you are beyond the need of God's grace."[15]

Christ is our righteousness, and he is the same yesterday and today and forever (Heb. 13:8). So we dare not place our trust in the best day ever or the sweetest frame of emotions; neither should we tremble because we had the worst day ever and the sourest disposition.

We delight in Jesus, who has become to us wisdom from God, our righteousness and sanctification and redemption (1 Cor. 1:30). Our delight in Jesus overflows into praise, and the Spirit bears his fruit in our lives so that God gets the glory.

"Time of Need?" That's *All* the Time in My House!

Frustrated moms and desperate housewives can draw near to God's throne of grace every day. We don't have to wait until the next no-good, very bad day.

Jesus our great high priest is at the Father's right hand pleading for us helpless sinners who trust the sacrifice he made on the cross on our behalf. "Let us then with confidence draw near to the throne of grace, that we may receive mercy and find grace to help in time of need" (Heb. 4:16).

A friend of mine once commented, " 'Time of need?' That's *all* the time in my house!" There's no better time than all the time to boldly ask God for mercy and grace. Your Father cares for you, Jesus has not abandoned you, and the Spirit assures our heart (Rom. 5:5).

Is the Lord your shepherd? He will not leave you wanting. God gives us this stewardship of grace according to his riches in glory in Christ Jesus, and he empowers us to do what he's called us to do. Every day!

Motherhood is physically exhausting, emotionally draining work. Where can a mother find the strength she needs to serve her family? From God, who is "able to make all grace abound to you, so that having all sufficiency in all things at all times, you may abound in every good work" (2 Cor. 9:8). Even when our back gives out and our body is tired, God can strengthen mothers "with all power, according to his glorious might, for all endurance and patience with joy" (Col. 1:11). Thanksgiving is the proper response to God as he extends to us all the inheritance of grace we have in Christ (Col. 1:12).

So while you're breathless from the hard work, you are breathing—a cause for praise! When you feel desperate for relief, it's a reminder that you are desperate for God's grace. Thank the Lord for the gift of feeling your need for him. Do you know where you are right now? You may be reading this book while sitting in your Honda Odyssey as you wait to pick up your kids from school. But do you know where you are? Have you been raised with Christ? You are in Christ, seated in the heavenly places with him. Then set your mind on the things that are above, where Christ is (Col. 3:2). Do you belong to him who has been raised from the dead? Bear fruit for God (Rom. 7:4). When your day is too much for you to handle and things feel like they're spinning out of control, take a deep breath and remind yourself: "Our God is a God of salvation, and to GOD, the LORD, belong deliverances from death" (Ps. 68:20). There are blood-bought promises that are yours to help you in these particular moments. Every day that the sun rises and sets can serve as a reminder to us that a day is coming when God's will is done on earth as it is in heaven. In all these ways and many more, mothers can receive God's kingdom even in the midst of their busy lives.

Better Than One More Kiss Goodnight

Everyone in our home who is under 4 feet tall tends to go a little bananas around 7:00 p.m. A wise friend often reminds me that someday I will have to convince my teenaged children to wake up and get out of their beds. Those days seem so far away.

Little children tend to feel most vulnerable at night. It's dark outside, the activity of the house is winding down, and they hear the bedtime no-more refrain: no more sippy cups, no more snacks, no more games, no more toys, no more cartwheels.

And then, cue the chorus response of bedtime one-mores: One more book? One more sip of water? One more hug? One more kiss goodnight?

By God's grace, the Holy Spirit's fruit of patience and gentleness swells and ripens in these times. God gets the glory for giving me the strength I need to be kind to my children when I feel hurried or annoyed at the end of a very long day.

And in times when I let the Spirit's fruit rot because of my sinfulness, the Lord gives me the grace I need to apologize to my kids for my hastiness, insensitivity, and unkind words. Bedtime is a maturing experience for all of us.

I assure my children of my presence. "Mommy is only going to the living room, and then I'm going to sleep in my bedroom. I'm right here." I leave them reminders and things to help them sleep: "Here's Judson's sheriff and spaceman, here's Aliza's rose pillow, and here's Norah's unicorn—and wombat, and bracelets, oh, and dolls. I left your music on the timer, and the bathroom light is on in case you need to go."

I give them extra affection to show them I love them: "Another kiss for you, and you, and you. And another hug for you, and you, and you."

Even so, the sniffles and protests might crescendo. I repeat one last verse as a reminder for them of God's presence and his fatherly care: "You can go to sleep with confidence because the Lord never sleeps and he is taking care of you. Even the darkness is as daylight to him, so he can always see you. If you feel anxious, then you pray to God and tell him all about it because he loves you so much, and he can help you."

But ultimately I have to leave. I have to give one last bedtime kiss, say one final goodnight, and close their door. What would my kids think is way better than all of these external assurances of my love and care for them? An internal, abiding presence. In their room, specifically: "Mommy, why don't you stay longer? Or sleep in our room?" They are most assured by my ongoing presence.

This bedtime cacophony is a glimpse of grace that reminds me that part of the Holy Spirit's ministry to me is to calm my anxious fears and give me peace and security when I feel uncertain of God's care and love.

The sealing of our soul for God is an effectual, unimpeachable work of the Spirit. For various reasons there are times when believers do not feel particularly close to God, yet we remain in Christ because of the Holy Spirit's indwelling presence. The Holy Spirit doesn't tolerate any "roommates" when he takes up residence in you. He can never be served an eviction notice; his tenancy is permanent. I began to appreciate this assurance more when reflecting on the testimonies of believers in Christ who had been previously influenced or possessed by unclean spirits. Dead in their trespasses and submitted to the wills of unclean spirits, these men and women behaved in accordance with the unclean, ungodly character of the spirit that occupied their "house." When the Holy Spirit took up permanent residence in them, they were sealed forever. Likewise, if you are in Christ, then the Spirit's presence is your assurance that you are sealed and marked for your heavenly Father forever. The Spirit is God, and his unalterable, effective work is an objective reality that can neither be negated nor confirmed by your subjective emotions (Eph. 1:13–15) nor threatened by any unclean spirit.

Surely our hearts are emboldened by the reminders and evidences we see of God's love for us all around. We see God's common grace, his divine providence, and so much more!

Even when we feel that we're going a little bananas because of this or that feeling of uncertainty or vulnerability, we can enjoy the abiding, internal assurance we receive from the Holy Spirit (Isa. 59:21), who pours out God's love into our hearts. What lengths the Lord has gone to so that our uncertain hearts might be comforted by his love!

With this perspective on our true hope and the source of our comfort, we can see the brilliance of Paul's prayer and ask the Lord that he would do the same for us: "May the Lord direct your hearts to the love of God and to the steadfastness of Christ" (2 Thess. 3:5).

Reflection

There are no perfect moms, but we'll die trying to prove we might be the exception. Is this your own admission as well?

If so, you likely know the accompanying feeling of being overwhelmed much of the time. But perfectionist spirit aside, mothering is just plain overwhelming at times. That's why we should consider this: "What is our hope when a deluge of domestic frustrations threatens to sweep us away into the sea of despondency?" There is hope—not just for some future season of life but right now.

1. We are all tempted to believe the lie that how well a day goes is a measure of how God feels about us. How does Romans 8:28–39 debunk that lie?

2. How does God use frustrating circumstances to grow us spiritually (see pp. 117–18)?

3. What does it mean that Christ is our righteousness (see Rom. 3:9–31)? How do Paul's words in Romans liberate us in our mothering?

4. Getting the kids to bed is an ongoing challenge for many mothers. Perhaps you can relate! What perspective helps enable us to face bedtime with peace (see pp. 121–23)?

5. There are times when believers don't feel particularly close to God (pp. 123–24). What reality contradicts those feelings? Review Romans 8:31–39; Ephesians 1:13–14; and 2 Thessalonians 3:5.

Going Deeper

Jerry Bridges's book *The Disciplines of Grace: God's Role and Our Role in the Pursuit of Holiness*[16] is a good resource for mothers who struggle with the sin of perfectionism. Studying it with a group of mothers would be an excellent way to follow up your study of *Treasuring Christ When Your Hands Are Full.*

9

The Fictitious Mother
of the Year

ONE YEAR AT CHRISTMAS I accidentally threw away the gingerbread cookie that my daughter had painstakingly decorated. She was so upset with me that I heard about the gingerbread incident until well past New Year's. I suppose that at the same time I fumbled the cookie into the trash, I threw away my nomination for Mother of the Year as well. Of course there is not a real "Mother of the Year" award, but we talk about it as we would a lighthearted joke. The reality, though, is that every mother fails to image God perfectly in her mothering. What doesn't seem so lighthearted is the feeling of guilt we experience when we honestly consider our inadequacies.

And the Nominees Are Not . . .

What mother isn't plagued by her feelings of inadequacy and guilt over her mistakes? A friend of mine told me that she has made it a rule to avoid gatherings of mothers because she feels overwhelmed by all of the "perfection" she sees. One can sympathize with her feelings. Imagining a room full of people whose presentation of their lives draws out your feelings of insecurity and guilt would make even the most confident person feel self-conscious.

Even those of us who rarely have thoughts of self-consciousness naturally sense our inadequacy to measure up to God's holiness. And rightly so. The Lord graciously created us with a conscience that bears witness to this very idea—not one of us is "good" by God's standards.

Even if we haven't committed any gross infractions that we're aware of, we don't have to look very far into our heart to uncover our sinfulness. We use our children to bloat our egos and make us look good. We criticize other mothers to alleviate our feelings of insecurity. We fail to love our children with selfless, sacrificial love. We neglect our children in the name of ministry. We break fellowship with our Christian sisters over petty matters of parenting preferences. We set bad examples and train our children to value the world's opinion over God's. And these are just a few of the ways we fail to live righteously.

There are also the other impossible standards that we invent and hold ourselves to. We feel shame over projects we start and don't finish. We feel guilty that our children aren't "turning out" as we had planned. We stumble into the snare of "the fear of man" and live for the approval of other mothers. We get angry over dreams of mothering perfection that could have been. We are our own harshest critics, meting out punishment for crimes against our fragile egos. In looking over this list, I realize that it wasn't too hard to come up with; I'm well acquainted with these issues. When I look back at my mothering track record, there are more flukes and failures than fantastic feats of faith.

What hope does a flawed mom have?

Against the backdrop of this bleak outlook, the gospel shines brighter and gives a more durable hope than the empty promises of self-actualization and the short-lived encouragement from glass-half-full optimism. The gospel changes how we view our failures, and we see how God redeems our flaws for his own glory. God has delivered the Christian mother from the domain of darkness and transferred her to the kingdom of his beloved Son, in whom she has redemption and the forgiveness of sin (Col. 1:13). In the gospel we hear about how we have grace for today and bright hope for tomorrow.

The gospel of grace says that God accepts you in Christ, and then he gives you his Son's righteous standing as a gift by faith. We don't first make ourselves holy so that God will then accept us. Our position in Christ lets loose a whole host of joys that transform our mothering. Among those joys is experiencing the indomitable power of the indwelling Holy Spirit to resist temptation and flee from sin. But before we go there, let's celebrate just how firm our foundation of justification by faith really is.

The Cross Aired All Your Dirty Laundry

We rise to defend ourselves over petty things. We give disclaimers about things such as how much we paid for something, why a child responded in a certain way, or why the kitchen countertop is a mess. We also justify things that are a big deal—like our sin. We don the theater mask of self-righteousness to cover up the lurid evil in our hearts. We scrub our guilty consciences with the soiled rags of our good deeds.

> We have all become like one who is unclean,
>   and all our righteous deeds are like a polluted
>   garment.

We all fade like a leaf,
  and our iniquities, like the wind, take us away.
    (Isa. 64:6)

The Bible says that pretending we have no sin is pointless, because the cross has already announced to the world just how guilty we are. We need a Savior, not a self-help guru. Our "dirtiest laundry" has already been aired. Our sin has offended an infinitely holy God so that the death of the perfect Son of God was required in order to rescue us from the eternal punishment that we deserve. That's why Jesus died in our place on the cross. The grace given to us through the cross liberates us from the heavy burden of pretense before other people and (most importantly) before God.

Through the gospel, God does something better for us than merely denying our guilt. God removes from us our filthy rags and clothes us in the righteousness of Christ.

I will greatly rejoice in the LORD;
  my soul shall exult in my God,
for he has clothed me with the garments of salvation;
  he has covered me with the robe of righteousness,
as a bridegroom decks himself like a priest with a
    beautiful headdress,

and as a bride adorns herself with her jewels.
(Isa. 61:10)

Sister, that means you can *rest*! You can lay aside any notion of working for God's approval and rest in Christ. Your righteous standing before God is something Christ has accomplished and always maintains for you. There's not a single thing that anyone can do to alter what Jesus has done. This grace frees us from the bondage of sin and the heavy burden of pretense and propels us to share with others how they can be freed too.

So why do we hide from God? Why do we numb our souls with our anesthetic of choice to try to shake off the conviction of the Holy Spirit? Why do we sweat and strain under the burden of pretense in front of friends who were saved by the same grace given to them by the same Savior, or in front of friends who don't know that grace can free them too? We have no good reason to shrink back from confessing our sins to the Lord or to our trustworthy sisters in Christ. We have every reason to glory in the cross and trust Jesus with our PR department. Milton Vincent says about the grace of the cross: "With the worst facts about me thus exposed to the view of others, I find myself feeling that I truly have nothing left to hide."[17] John Bunyan describes our justification as a great mystery: "And, indeed, this is one of the greatest mysteries in the world; namely, that a righteousness that resides in heaven should justify me, a sinner on earth!"[18] This is an exuberant mystery indeed!

If you are in Christ, then there is no sin that you can commit for which the punishment has not already been dealt with on the cross. We suffer consequences for our sin—broken relationships, physical injury, a damaged reputation, and the like. But even so, your justification in Christ is intact. God will not and does not change his mind. He knew the worst things about you and he knew your self-righteous tendencies when he declared you righteous for Jesus's sake.

The verdict is in, sister: Jesus paid it all. We're righteous in Christ, forgiven of our sins, and free to love the Lord and our neighbor as Jesus has loved us (John 13:34), as Christ's love controls us (2 Cor. 5:14). We can throw off the sin that so easily entangles us, and we can run with endurance this adventure in motherhood that God has given us. We don't live for ourselves anymore, but we live for him who died for our sake and was raised (2 Cor. 5:15). This is more than just good news for us; it's good news for our children and the other mothers we spend time with. Instead of being preoccupied with building our own kingdoms, we can take up the ministry of reconciliation that God has given us. "Therefore we are ambassadors for Christ, God making his appeal through us.

We implore you on behalf of Christ, be reconciled to God. For our sake he made him to be sin who knew no sin, so that in him we might become the righteousness of God" (2 Cor. 5:20–21). When you discover that you are the unworthy recipient of God's lavish grace, you cannot help but share it with others.

Even Super Mom Needs God's Grace

Advice on things such as choosing a safe car seat or teaching a finicky preschooler to eat a well-balanced meal is easy to come by. Instructions on how to love your neighbor and nurture your children are also readily available. What we are less likely to come by is encouragement to consider how the gospel transforms our motherhood.

My prideful heart wants so badly to be Super Mom and for other moms to think I'm Super Mom. Sometimes I prefer to glory in things other than God's grace. Pride shows up in many forms. When we're tempted to revel in the acceptance of others, we need to draw near to God's throne of grace. We can have confidence that God will hear our prayers, come to our aid, and bolster our hope in him because of what Christ has done for us on the cross. Pride induces us to worry about tomorrow as though we can control the outcome with our anxiety. In those hand-wringing moments we need to remember that God's grace will still be sufficient tomorrow. That means we have all the grace we need for now. And when later becomes now, God will give us the grace we need in that moment too. God's future grace in Christ is more real than all of the anxiety-ridden hypothetical situations that threaten to keep us awake tonight.

Pride shows up in our interactions with our children too. For example, in frustration-filled moments we demean our children for mere childishness, insinuating that at that moment there is no grace available for them. Instead of marveling together with them at the grace we all need, we dole out guilt for their young consciences to carry. Our proud hearts are reticent to surrender to the grace of God that is given for us *and* for our children.

I know my pride lives in a house of mirrors. I catch glimpses of myself in my sin and balk: *I knew better! This isn't the real me. The real me just needed to be reminded to be the best me that I know that I am.* Do you struggle with this too? More than ever, when we hear ourselves proudly justifying our sin, we must resist the lie that says our deepest need is forgetfulness. We need a Savior! The gospel speaks of Jesus, who is the only one who truly loved his neighbor. Christ's precious blood is the means through which our sin is atoned—not through denial or delusional self-justification. As women who want to boast in our weaknesses, serve with Christ's strength, and rejoice in the blood of Christ that covers all our sins, we have a few pointed questions to ask ourselves:

- Why do we try to wrestle back from Christ some of the shame he endured for our sake?
- Why do we want to take back the burden of our guilt that Jesus bore on the cross just so we can chase a shadow of self-righteous dignity?
- Do we really mean to say that our sin is beyond the reach of God's transforming grace?
- Do we really dare to suggest that the work of Christ on the cross is not sufficient to cover our foibles, follies, and failures as a mother?
- Do we really dare to hand back to God his declarative sentence—"This sinner is *justified*!"—so that we can wander a bit longer in Mommy Purgatory?

Surely God's grace is infinitely more lovely and utterly irresistible than any vainglory we can entertain. "Grace burst forth spontaneously from the bosom of eternal love and rested not until it had removed every impediment and found its way to the sinner's side, swelling round him in full flow. Grace does away with the distance between the sinner and

God, which sin had created. Grace meets the sinner on the spot where he stands; grace approaches him just as he is."[19]

Arise, My Soul, Arise

Our assurance is not based on knowing the right things to do and thinking we would do better if given the chance. No amount of self-deprecating or good intentions can atone for sin before a holy God. No, we are represented by a surety, someone who has willingly taken the full legal responsibility for our insurmountable sin debt with God. Jesus is our "guarantor" (Heb. 7:22). And our surety now stands before the throne of God—his bleeding sacrifice for sins pleads for God's grace (Heb. 12:24).

Sinclair Ferguson said in his book *In Christ Alone*,

When I know that Christ is the one real sacrifice for my sins, that His work on my behalf has been accepted by God, that He is my heavenly Intercessor—then His blood is the antidote to the poison in the voices that echo in my conscience, condemning me for my many failures. Indeed, Christ's shed blood chokes them into silence![20]

Guilt is a terrible motivator, and guilt never strengthened anyone's heart. In Christ alone we can be certain of full forgiveness today and certain of more grace tomorrow. The indignant, self-righteous lament, "I know better than this; how could I have been so foolish?" is a poor conduit of grace in our lives and offers us nothing for tomorrow but compounded guilt. But the soul-freeing news of the gospel that says Jesus loved us perfectly on the cross and redeems our failures—this news is of another kind. This is very good news. Now *with faith-filled joy* we can rejoice in God and say, "How could I have been so foolish? See the grace he has shown me in his Son!" Do you see your need for Jesus? Run to him! Waste no time. Jesus's blood forgives us of our insurmountable sin mortgage and releases us from the chains of our delusional self-righteousness. We are free to walk in God's love and love our neighbors with the strength that he supplies. We can sing with Charles Wesley, "Arise, my soul, arise; shake off your guilty fears and rise!" As we rise, we rise with fear and trembling that God—the God who threw the stars into place—is able to work in us and is pleased to do so.

As we rise, we rise to God, who executed his judgment on his Son for us and brings us out into his light (Mic. 7:8–9). We approach his throne with confidence to claim the grace that is now guaranteed us in Christ. Then by God's grace we can extend grace to our children.

Don't Give Up

God has decreed that those who are in Christ will stand in a righteousness that is not their own. "There is therefore now no condemnation for those who are in Christ Jesus" (Rom. 8:1). God our Father, who disciplines us because he loves us (Prov. 3:11–12), is the same God who is for us interminably to the end (Rom. 8:38–39). It is the Lord who is able to make us stand as mothers whose hearts are fully his. We have confidence in Christ in the face of anything that impotently threatens to try to separate us from his love. "Rejoice not over me, O my enemy; when I fall, I shall rise; when I sit in darkness, the LORD will be a light to me" (Mic. 7:8). We magnify the grace of God when we serve our families with all our might, even though we are beset with weaknesses, frailty, timidity, and faithlessness. The Lord, who disciplines those he loves, will be your irresistible advocate, and he will triumph in court for you. He will plead your case. He will be your light. The cloud will pass. And you will stand in a righteousness that is not your own and do the work he has given you to do. Oh, let us learn the secret of gutsy guilt from the steadfastness of sinful saints who were not paralyzed by their imperfections. God has a great work for everyone to do. Mother your children with all your might—yes, and even with all your flaws and all your sins. And in the obedience of this faith, magnify the glory of his grace and do not grow weary in doing good.

You and I may never be nominated for the fictitious Mother of the Year award. The proverbial trophy case could remain empty. But, really, we don't need a trophy to commemorate our service in motherhood. In order to glory in Christ's power, we don't necessarily even need our children to rise up and call us blessed (though that would be nice). The boasting we want to do in our motherhood is of a more radical sort. We want to boast *all the more gladly* of our weaknesses and need for God's grace so that Christ's power will rest on us (2 Cor. 12:9).

Consider Christ's atonement, the gift of justification and imputed righteousness, and Jesus's priestly intercession for you. Resist the urge to grow weary and give up (Gal. 6:9). Glorify God by enjoying him—he is a truer and better award than the adulations of our children, of other women, and even of our self-approval.

Reflection

Many mothers are plagued by feelings of inadequacy and guilt over their mistakes. Feelings of insecurity can lead us to act unkindly and to try to cover up our weaknesses, but that only compounds our guilt. The good news is that God doesn't cover up our flaws—he actually covers them, and he does so completely by the blood of Christ. Then he redeems our failures for his glory.

1. We all have a tendency to use our children "to bloat our egos and make us look good" (p. 128). In what particular ways is this a temptation for you?

2. The fear of man is a very real danger. Living in its grip can impact both our children and our enjoyment of God's fellowship. What underlies our pull toward the fear of man (see Prov. 29:25 and Jer. 17:5–8)?

3. "Our 'dirtiest laundry' has already been aired" (p. 131). How, according to Isaiah 61:10, can admitting the truth of our sin actually lead us to rejoice?

4. This chapter focuses on our justification in Christ. What exactly does *justification* mean? What are some of the ways it can impact both our mothering and how we view ourselves?

5. Grace is greater than pride, but pride so often rules us. Where does pride tend to show up in our lives? How can we humble our hearts and thoughts to allow grace to permeate and conquer our pride? Use the Scripture references quoted in this chapter as the basis for your answer, and then apply those truths specifically to your life.

6. There is a list of questions to ask ourselves on page 135. How would you answer these questions today?

Going Deeper

"Guilt is a terrible motivator, and guilt never strengthened anyone's heart" (p. 137). What insights into our guilt do we get from the prophet Zechariah's vision (Zech. 3:1–5)? How does Ephesians 6:10–20 serve as a practical follow-up to what we learn from Zechariah's vision?

10

Mothers Are Weak,
but He Is Strong

ONE MORNING BEFORE my three kids greeted the sun with
their exuberant declarations of love for the wee hours of the
day, I was typing some notes for the manuscript of this book.
Fatigued, yet eager to study more about God's mercy for us as
mothers, I was cocooned under a blanket on the couch with
my laptop and some coffee. Then I suddenly became aware
of the fact that my morning coffee tasted to me like motor
oil and soap scum.

"Is this really real? Could it be?" My heart started beating
faster.

I wondered if my taste buds were lying. My hand already
sweating, I lifted my mug to take another sip. Yes, it tasted

like motor oil and soap scum brewed together and masquerading as something delicious and comforting. So I dumped the foul-tasting coffee down the drain and rinsed my mouth with some water.

I heard my girls discussing what their baby brother should wear that day, so I went in to their bedroom and intervened on his behalf. After breakfast my husband kissed us all goodbye, and he headed downstairs to catch a taxi to go to work.

"Shoes on everybody!" I announced, and we ditched our usual morning routine to go on an outing. We marched down the hallway, went down the elevator to the ground level, and marched across the street to the pharmacy. I had to find out if my suspicions were true.

And they were. It was really real. Baby number four was on the way!

Overwhelming feelings of gladness mingled with fear upon this discovery. Another child! I felt so unworthy of such a great gift from God. Yet at the same time my heart quaked because of the awesome reality of the responsibility and work that another baby would bring. Just that week my husband had asked me to specially pray for his joy and for pain relief because his chronic arm pain was the worst he had experienced in a long time. My mind wandered back to familiar old doubts: *What if things continued to get worse and worse for David's health? What then? Can God sustain our family through chronic pain and everything that comes with it plus a new baby?* The temptation to doubt God's perfect will felt almost tangible. But so did the assurance of the indwelling Holy Spirit who spoke to my heart, "Oh give thanks to the LORD, for he is good; for his steadfast love endures forever!" (1 Chron. 16:34).

I remembered that motherhood is not a blessing given to me because I deserve it. It isn't a reward for my good deeds or (as some might suggest) a sentencing for my bad deeds. God made me a mother because he jealously and rightly desires praise for his own name, and this is how he saw fit to do it. God aims to glorify himself through my family, and we all get to be carried along by his grace. He has created these children, in these circumstances, for such a time as this. God is so very good. His goodness is not a shifting shadow of a changeable attitude but an unchanging attribute. Everything God has for us in Jesus is a gift of his mercy. And so by God's grace, while trembling yet trusting, I praised the Lord for his generous gift of new life!

Christian mother, all of us need to remember whose we are and who he says we are. God has plans to glorify himself in your life that are beyond what you can imagine.

The Illusion of Strength

While we might acknowledge that the work of mothering is demanding and difficult, sometimes we live as though we don't need any help. Spoken as a testimony to a woman's strength, we hear that "motherhood is not for the faint of heart."

However, a case can be made that motherhood is *only* for the faint of heart. When the first child was born, Eve said, "I have gotten a man with the help of the Lord" (Gen. 4:1). On occasion in my doula work, a woman will admit to me that she doesn't think she can do it—endure to the end of her pregnancy, give birth to her baby, or raise her child. When we acknowledge our inability to mother our children apart from the Lord's provision and strength, we honor God. *Of course* we are not able to do this work of raising children and training them in the instruction of the Lord. That's why we desperately need the Lord! We are to "be strong in *the Lord* and in the strength of *his might*" (Eph. 6:10).

This kind of absolute dependency on God insults our pride. We're so quick to embrace other solutions for our emotional, physical, and mental fatigue. "I can figure this out on my own," we tell ourselves. More often than not in our trials we pretend everything is okay, and we dive headlong into self-sufficiency. Faith, rather, acknowledges the fierceness of the storm and throws us into the sea, and we swim as fast as we can to where we see Jesus walking on the water (John 6:16–21).

Physically, emotionally, mentally, and spiritually, we need the Lord's strength to honor him in our motherhood. Sometimes the pitter-patter of little feet means that your child is running a marker along the wall in the hallway while he toddles away from you. The sweet, bleating cries of a newborn can turn into sassy comebacks and spiteful words. In every occasion, moms must rely on God's strength. If we think we can do "this motherhood thing" in our own strength, then we are fooling ourselves.

A few summers ago I saw an orthopedic doctor for some troubling lower back pain I was having. I couldn't lean over to change a diaper without my back freezing up, and it ached even after a good night's rest. After a physical examination and some X-rays the doctor diagnosed my problem. "Your strength is spent!" he said. "When was the last time you did any core-strengthening exercises?" "Dr. Candid" explained that my back muscles were struggling to make up for my weak abdominal muscles. He prescribed some painkillers for when my back was really in pain, and he gave me some valuable advice: "If you don't do some sit-ups soon, then you're going to do more serious damage to your back." His frankness startled me, but he was right. I'm glad he told me the truth about my pain and encouraged me to do what I could to strengthen my body. My physical strength had been an illusion, and finding out about this was a good wake-up call to be disciplined.

Parenting When Your Strength Is Spent

A dear friend of mine who has a married daughter, a college graduate, and a high school graduate likes to remind me, "Your physical strength is spent when your kids are young, and then when they get older your emotional strength fails you too." As our children grow, we never outgrow our need for God's moment-to-moment grace through the gospel. Disciplining ourselves to consciously depend on his strength is the way we grow in faith.

Whenever I consider my motherhood, I usually turn to a mental list of all the ways I wish I could do more for my kids. I want to pray more consistently for them, be more intentional in instructing them in the Lord's ways, kiss and hug them more, and remember to feed them their multivitamins every day. These are good goals to have, but when my sights are on my limited strength, my work is a burden and not a grace-empowered joy.

In the English Standard Version of the Bible the subtitle for Psalm 71 is this: "Forsake Me Not When My Strength Is Spent." This is profoundly descriptive of a psalm that lauds the Lord as the one who saves us in his righteousness and is to us a rock of refuge. Whether you feel that you just can't endure or that you don't "have it in you" anymore, or if you feel that you've "got what it takes," the gospel triumphs over all. Only God's grace in the gospel can strengthen our faith to let Jesus carry our burdens in parenting.

Talk to Yourself

One of the ways to have your faith strengthened is to renew your mind continually by meditating on the truths of the gospel. Talk to yourself about what God's word says. Remind yourself and your children often of who God is, what he has done to save sinners through Jesus's death on the cross, and how through the guarantee of the indwelling Spirit he has shown us his commitment to keep us until the end.

Are you feeling quite put together today? Be humbled as you remind yourself of who it was that put you together in the first place and sustains your very life. "For you formed my inward parts; you knitted me together in my mother's womb" (Ps. 139:13).

Are you feeling overwhelmed by your weakness? Boast in God's power to use you despite your weakness. "But he said to me, 'My grace is sufficient for you, for my power is made perfect in weakness.' Therefore I will boast all the more gladly of my weaknesses, so that the power of Christ may rest upon me" (2 Cor. 12:9). Remember Christ, your surety, stands *for you*.

> When the avenger of blood follows you, flee immediately to this sanctuary. Think: Let me not deny myself comfort and God glory both at once. "Where sin abounds, grace abounds much more" (Rom. 5:20). Though sins after conversion stain our profession more than sins before conversion, go still to the glorious mercy of God. To seventy times seventy times, there is yet mercy. We beseech you be reconciled, said St. Paul to the Corinthians, when they were in the state of grace and already had their pardon. Let us never be discouraged from going to Christ.[21]

The gospel has relevance to your day today no matter how strong you feel at this moment. The response we should have to this news is overflowing praise so that others can see how good the Lord is to you.

My mouth will tell of your righteous acts,
 of your deeds of salvation all the day,
 for their number is past my knowledge.
With the mighty deeds of the Lord God I will come;
 I will remind them of your righteousness, yours
  alone. . . .

So even to old age and gray hairs,
 O God, do not forsake me,
until I proclaim your might to another generation,
  your power to all those to come.
Your righteousness, O God,
 reaches the high heavens.
You who have done great things,
 O God, who is like you? (Ps. 71:15–19)

Serve with the Strength God Provides

The Lord tells us through Peter that we should not serve in our own strength. God tells us this because we have no strength with which we might serve him in the first place.

As each has received a gift, use it to serve one another, as good stewards of God's varied grace: whoever speaks, as one who speaks oracles of God; whoever serves, as one who serves by the strength that God supplies—in order that in everything God may be glorified through Jesus Christ. To him belong glory and dominion forever and ever. Amen. (1 Pet. 4:10–11).

Jesus died on the cross so that we would have the free, unmerited grace of God. And as we appropriate that grace in our lives and serve others, we are serving in the strength God supplies. This is how we can serve so that God gets the glory—through his strength because of his grace shown to us in Jesus.

God's grace is sufficient for everything he has called us to. "And God is able to make all grace abound to you, so that having all sufficiency in all things at all times, you may abound in every good work" (2 Cor. 9:8). God makes all grace abound to us through his Son, Jesus. And it's through the strength of the indwelling Holy Spirit that we are able to abound in (not just drag through) every good work he lays in front of us. And as we work, we work with an eye toward eternity, knowing that our work is not in vain in the Lord. "Therefore, my beloved brothers, be steadfast, immovable, always abounding in the work of the Lord, knowing that in the Lord your labor is not in vain" (1 Cor. 15:58).

Even as we are trembling and trusting in the Lord, God makes us worthy of his calling and fulfills every resolve for good and every work of faith by *his* power (2 Thess. 1:11). According to his grace, God glorifies the name of our Lord Jesus in mothers who serve by the strength he supplies.

———

Reflection

Because our perspective is limited, we easily forget that God has plans to glorify himself in and through our lives—plans that are beyond anything we can imagine. Even when we do remember, we wonder how it will ever happen. We just know ourselves too well! But that's exactly where the gospel comes in. At the end of the day, it's not up to us. And it's not about us. It's all about him, and we live out our calling to his glory through the strength he supplies.

1. Explain the meaning of "motherhood is *only* for the faint of heart" (p. 146).

2. What is the biggest obstacle to our depending fully on God? Why is that obstacle really only an illusion? Following from this, what is the primary way we grow in faith (see pp. 146–48)?

3. Where are you feeling especially weak at present? Review 2 Corinthians 12:7–10. How can you see God at work in the "thorn" of your particular weakness?

4. The apostle Peter instructs us about Christian service, whether done in the home or the church:

   As each has received a gift, use it to serve one another, as good stewards of God's varied grace: whoever speaks, as one who speaks oracles of God; whoever serves, as one who serves by the strength that God supplies—in order that in everything God may be glorified through Jesus Christ. To him belong glory and dominion forever and ever. Amen. (1 Pet. 4:10–11)

   According to Peter, how are we to serve, and what is the ultimate purpose of all our service?

5. What encouragement to persevere through the difficult aspects of motherhood is offered in 1 Corinthians 15:58 and 2 Thessalonians 1:11? In each verse we are both instructed and freed. How?

Going Deeper

Psalm 71 "lauds the Lord as the one who saves us in his righteousness and is to us a rock of refuge." Work through the psalm and note all of the following:

The psalmist's concerns. What is causing him trouble?

The psalmist's petitions. What does he ask God to do?

The psalmist's commitments. What does he vow to do?

The psalmist's reasons for trust. What attributes of God does he put forth?

11

The Big Story of Motherhood

CULTURES ACROSS the globe recognize that motherhood is honorable.

We once ate at a popular barbeque joint in Syracuse, New York. Seated at the table next to us was a biker with an elaborate "I Love Mom" tattoo on his bicep. When I spent some time in Mombasa, Kenya, I watched people clear out spaces on the crowded *mutatus* (a kind of bus/taxi) to make room for mothers. A few years ago when my own mother and my husband's mother came to visit us here in the Middle East, our fellow church members honored them with encouragement and praise. In this global city filled with the nations, I can't count all the times I've been out and about and received special treatment from people simply because I am a mother. When I am pregnant, my husband particularly enjoys when waiters gift us with free dessert "for the baby." When one hears a story of how a mother was mistreated or given a hard time, there is often a visceral reaction of injustice or shame. In observing people from various cultures here, I've noticed how failing to honor your mother will earn you the title of "ingrate."

Motherhood Is a Precious Gift

Yet even as we make much of motherhood, some statements we hear about it tend to sound insincere and trite. I remember acutely feeling this way as I struggled to change an explosive diaper on my lap on an airplane, and the older gentleman next to me commented, "Isn't motherhood such a blessing?" I had to ask myself if he was sincere, or making a lighthearted joke, or if he was being disdainfully sarcastic.

If motherhood is a gift, then why does the true blessedness of motherhood elicit in us such skepticism?

I think one of the reasons I wrestle with this is my sin. I need to be transformed by the renewing of my worldly mind so that I can discern God's good and perfect will (Rom. 12:2). Without God's work of sanctification in my life, I would be left in my sinful thinking that both idolizes *and* despises motherhood. I can easily turn motherhood into something that's all about me or even downplay it to the degree that it is pitiable.

The Bible describes motherhood as neither a diminishing of a woman's personhood nor the sum of her personhood. Womanhood, ultimately, is about a different person altogether. Likewise, motherhood is about a different person all together. The highest aim of womanhood is not motherhood; the highest aim of womanhood is being conformed to the image of Christ. The multifaceted goal of motherhood points us in the same direction. One of the gifts of motherhood is that God uses it to trace the image of his Son onto our lives.

When we make motherhood (or anything else) all about us, we eventually get bored. And of course we get bored with motherhood when we obsess over it, because motherhood was never meant to fully satisfy us. When we get bored we get cynical: "Motherhood—a gift? *Right.*" Some women lament that if God ever gives them children, they will be devastated. Some women lament that if God never gives them children, they will be devastated. Should we be seeking a middle ground? Should Christian women just take a dose of cynicism and chase it down with a glass half full of gratitude as the world might suggest? I think the Bible gives us the answer to that question.

In Adam All Die

The Bible offers a paradigm for us to think about motherhood that is outside of our worldly ideals.

Perhaps, like me, you need a regular "note to self " from God's word regarding motherhood. It's crucial to remember what the Bible says when we battle our feelings of apathy or idolatrous desire regarding the gift of motherhood.

In Genesis 1:28 God blessed the man and woman he created. He said to them (among other things), "Be fruitful and multiply and fill the earth and subdue it." Subduing, ruling, multiplying—these are things that neither of them could do by themselves. These are things they could never do without God's help. God made male and female, both in his likeness, and then joined them together. He designed them to be utterly dependent on him for everything.

But Adam and Eve decided they did not need to depend on God for everything. *Who needs God's wisdom when you've got what it takes?* was their rationale. Consumed with themselves and eating the lie that the serpent hissed, the man and the woman disobeyed God and ate the forbidden fruit. They scoffed at death, which is God's just punishment for sin. *Yikes* is too weak of a word for this dilemma.

We've discussed this story in this book already, but its significance bears repeating. It's easy for us to feel removed from this incident in the garden. We were born into a world where we hear the preposterous idea that "death is a fact of life." What relevance does this incident in the garden of Eden have for our lives? The answer, in short, is that Adam's sin and death are connected to ours. "For as in Adam all die . . ." (1 Cor. 15:22). Hold that thought—now what? Specifically, *now what is to become of motherhood*? Would not the human race be justly extinguished because of the man and woman's cosmic treason against Almighty God?

Life in Spite of Death

Within the curse that God pronounced against the serpent, we can hear the reverberations of his heartbeat of mercy. He looks on Adam and Eve, who have become his enemies, and he has compassion on them. In the curse, God describes an epic war that will take place between the evil one and the offspring of the woman:

> I will put enmity between you and the woman,
>   and between your offspring and her offspring;
> he shall bruise your head,
>   and you shall bruise his heel. (Gen. 3:15)

The woman would have offspring.

The curse pronounced on the serpent is laden with God's mercy toward his children. The particular offspring whom God promised is Christ Jesus, our blessed hope. Satan would wound him; in the upside-down logic of strength through suffering, the Messiah would have the decisive victory in this war. Someday a Messiah would be born, and he would change the course of the universe forever.

Richard Sibbes said of this glimpse into the gospel,

> You know that promise that begets all others, "the seed of the woman" (Gen. 3:15). That repealed the curse and conveyed the mercy of God in Christ to Adam. So all the sweet and gracious promises have their source in that. All meet in Christ as in a centre; all are made for him and in him; he is the sum of all the promises. All the good things we have are parcels of Christ.[22]

Adam counted God's promise of life as good as done. "The man called his wife's name Eve, because she was the mother of all living" (Gen. 3:20). I want to hope in God like Adam did in that moment.

The fact of life is a global, historical, and eschatological demonstration of God's rich mercy. This was true in the garden, and it is true for us now. We draw breath by the grace and mercy of the Lord, who is not slow to fulfill his promise but is patient toward sinners, that we might repent and cherish him forever (2 Pet. 3:9).

Motherhood by Faith

Like Adam and Eve, we all deserve death because of our sin against God. And like Adam and Eve, our only hope is in the promised Messiah, who did for us what we could never and would never do for ourselves. Jesus put himself forward as a sacrifice for our sins, and he dealt the fatal blow to death and Satan.

By the power of his word, Jesus sustains the universe, including every child who has ever been conceived. Motherhood is God's conception—he ordained it and sustains it to the praise of his glorious grace. Life serves God's glory alone. Above and beyond the gift of physical life, which none of us deserves, our sovereign Lord Jesus holds out to us the hope of eternal life, which God, who never lies, promised before the ages began (Titus 1:2). When we trust in Christ, he joins us to himself, and he gives us this eternal life.

Being born again is neither drab nor stale. "For as in Adam all die, so also in Christ shall all be made alive" (1 Cor. 15:22). By faith we look backward to the cross, and we see the author of life bearing away our sins. By faith we look forward to the day when we will be face-to-face with our Lord forever. *As mothers nurture life by faith, they participate in the eschatological triumph of Christ's victory over sin and death.*

In eternity we will ever be acutely aware of how thrilling it is to be a recipient of God's grace because it gives us God. The very fact of life is evidence that the author of life is a God of mercy and grace and faithfulness. So when it feels as though your heart could just burst as you gaze on your sleeping baby, or as you sense a thrill of wonder when you scan the horizon of your city bustling with people, or as you marvel at pictures of God's image bearers the world over, erupt in praise to God. There's nothing boring about the concept of motherhood.

Even so, how quickly we can forget Jesus when the days and nights are full of good gifts from God. Too often we are happily circumscribed in our myopic little kingdom where we melt down signposts that point us to Jesus and fashion them into idols to worship.

Yet God's perfect character reassures us that he is greater than our weaknesses: "If we are faithless, he remains faithful— for he cannot deny himself" (2 Tim. 2:13). Christ our anchor rescues us from chasing after our vanities and releases us to use our gifts to build his everlasting kingdom instead. The fire of our hope in Christ is stoked by feeding on God's word, but not just so that we feel full. As we go about our mothering by God's grace, our hope in Christ becomes a witness to the people in our homes. Our satisfaction in Christ engenders even more satisfaction in Christ as we pour out our lives in service to others. When our hope is in Christ, those in our home are intrigued, and they want answers: What is the reason for the hope that is in you? (1 Pet. 3:15).

What Is the Goal of Motherhood?

Motherhood is a piece of evidence of God's triumphant agenda to give life despite the curse of death. It is a gift that points us to Jesus. As life marches on to the praise of God's glory, we see a riveting display of the grace of our Father, who will fulfill his promise to give his Son an inheritance of nations to the praise of his glory. There's no greater goal than that.

There are superfluous ideas circulating in the world that try to explain the goal of motherhood. Many of these ideas have a spiritual bend to them, describing motherhood as an expression of "the human spirit" or a metaphor for "Mother Earth." As Christians we understand that any spiritual guidance for motherhood that attempts to connect a woman to God apart from the substitutionary atoning death of Jesus cannot ultimately succeed. Jesus's claim to be "the way, and the truth, and the life" (John 14:6) has implications for the way we view our role as mothers. The lens of the profound reality of the gospel is where we see motherhood for what it is—a mercy. Praise God for the mercy he has on us even when we turn this gift into a vehicle for our self-fulfillment.

With Adam and Eve's sin in the garden, all their progeny along with them were justly indicted and condemned to death. Despite their grievous sin, God not only allowed life but facilitated it and sustains it still today. The mercy shown to us at the cross of Jesus Christ is the pinnacle of God's lavish grace. Herman Bavinck wrote, "Based on that sacrifice [Christ], God can wrench the world and humanity out of the grip of sin and expand his kingdom."[23]

Even while we steal God's glory and insist that motherhood exists to serve our egos and our reputations, God gives us more mercy still. Even while we wring our hands anxiously over God's timing for our families, God graciously continues to fulfill his eternal purposes in creating each and every member of our families. Relieved of our self-oriented passions, we can rejoice in the reconciliation we receive through Jesus, embrace God's purposes in our motherhood, and smile at the future as we look forward to the future grace that is ours in Christ Jesus. God designed motherhood to highlight his great mercy and point us to who we (and our children) were made for: the eternally satisfying risen Christ (John 17:24). The joys of today's motherhood are true joys, but they are like shadowy reflections in a mirror. At the end of every day—chaotic and mundane alike—motherhood is about the adoration and enjoyment of our great God. The seraphim in heaven continually cry out, "And one called to another and said: 'Holy, holy, holy is the Lord of hosts; the whole earth is full of his glory!'" (Isa. 6:3). We rejoice in motherhood today, as it is meant to direct us to worship God in everything we do, as a preamble to the worship we'll enjoy in heaven forever.

Even while we go about the exhausting work of motherhood that oftentimes feels so futile, we can be about what we're going to be about forever. In Revelation 5, John sees a vision of the risen Christ, glorified and reigning. In verse 13, John tells us how everyone responds to Jesus: "And I heard every creature in heaven and on earth and under the earth and in the sea, and all that is in them, saying, 'To him who sits on the throne and to the Lamb be blessing and honor and glory and might forever and ever!'" Forever in eternity we will be praising the Lord, and even now we can praise him as we know Jesus Christ and him crucified for us.

The next time something blasé happens, like the laundry filling up (again), or discovering what's left of (another) tissue box your toddler has curiously disemboweled, let your groaning turn into hallelujahs: "Praise the Lord, all nations! Extol him, all peoples! For great is his steadfast love toward us, and the faithfulness of the Lord endures forever. Praise the Lord!" (Ps. 117:1–2). Remind yourself of the truths in

God's word and be astonished as the Spirit reminds you of what your faith-eyes have seen.

> [Faith] is the noblest sight of all. And it is as quick as sight; for faith is that eagle in the cloud. It breaks through all and sees in a moment Christ in heaven; it looks backward and sees Christ upon the cross; it looks forward and sees Christ to come in glory. Faith is so quick a grace that it presents things past, things above and things to come—all in a moment, so quick is this eagle-eye of faith.[24]

Allow motherhood to incline your heart to worship, and bless the Lord who fills your hands with blessings. "I will extol you, my God and King, and bless your name forever and ever. Every day I will bless you and praise your name forever and ever. Great is the LORD, and greatly to be praised, and his greatness is unsearchable" (Ps. 145:1–3). Praising our great and merciful God is a mother's anthem—the song she'll be singing forever and ever.

Reflection

If being a mom is a gift, then why does the true blessedness of motherhood elicit in us such skepticism? The overarching reason is sin. Our sin skews our perspectives and focuses us inward rather than outward and upward. But skepticism drowns under the flood of God's grace and mercy as we view our calling through the lens of Scripture.

1. What we fixate on can shape the course of our life, which is why God's word calls us to govern our thoughts. Read Romans 12:1–2. What contrast is set for us in this passage? How are we transformed and renewed, and for what purposes?

2. "The highest aim of womanhood is not motherhood; the highest aim of womanhood is being conformed to the image of Christ." What happens when we seek to define ourselves by our motherhood? How have you experienced the reality of this in your own life?

3. In Genesis, God told Adam and Eve to be fruitful and multiply (1:28), but then sin entered in, and death became a fact of life. Yet there is mercy! How is mercy revealed in the curse God pronounced against the serpent (3:15) (see pp. 161–62)?

4. The apostle Peter writes, "In your hearts honor Christ the Lord as holy, always being prepared to make a defense to anyone who asks you for a reason for the hope that is in you" (1 Pet. 3:15). How does heeding Peter's instruction breed satisfaction (see pp. 164–65)?

5. What is the overarching purpose of motherhood (see pp. 165–67)? How does this purpose alter your outlook on the daily aspects of parenting?

Going Deeper

Motherhood is meant to direct our hearts to worship. Study Psalm 145, and list everything the Lord is praised for.

Conclusion

A Mother's Testimony of Peace

A REGULAR CONVERSATION in our home is about what other people are doing at that very moment in different parts of the world.

Our kids ask questions such as, "Whose time zones are sleeping right now?" "What are the children in India doing right now?" "Do you think our friends in Scotland are at school right now?" "Who is having a morning coffee right now?"

Perhaps the funniest question to date is: "*(sigh)* Do any other five-year-old girls in the world have to go sit in time-out right now?"

Talking about things like time zones and geography is a neat educational exercise for the kids. It also serves as a timely reminder to me of the steadfast love of the Lord and how his mercy never ends. All around the world, God is giving and sustaining life to the praise of his grace. His mercy is new every morning, and it's always morning somewhere. We need to be reminded of who God is every single day. John Owen reminds us of how the process of sanctification is just that—a process.

> The growth of trees and plants takes place so slowly that it is not easily seen. Daily we notice little change. But, in the course of time, we see that a great change has taken place. So it is with grace. Sanctification is a progressive, lifelong work (Prov. 4:18). It is an amazing work of God's grace, and it is a work to be prayed for (Rom. 8:27).[25]

Our hearts need to treasure Jesus, whom God appointed as heir of all things, who created all things, and who upholds the universe by the word of his power (Heb. 1:1–3). The little speck of rock that we're spinning around on amid the vast cosmos is being held together by Christ. It's good for us to humble ourselves and remember that even in all of its seemingly unsearchable brilliance, the universe is quite the understatement of Jesus's radiant glory. No one can fathom the scope of his greatness. "Oh, the depth of the riches and wisdom and knowledge of God! How unsearchable are his judgments and how inscrutable his ways!" (Rom. 11:33; see also Job 26 and Ps. 145:3).

In our moments of frustration, pride, and apathy it serves us well to remember that Jesus has been given all authority over everything (Ps. 8:6; Matt. 28:18; Eph. 1:22). Everything was created through him and for him (Col. 1:16). There is no thing or situation or circumstance that is more powerful than he is.

Meditating on God's character gives rise to great hope in our hearts, even in times of terrible trials. The occasion for the prophet Jeremiah's grief was Babylon's merciless destruction of Jerusalem. In the midst of unspeakable horror Jeremiah found cause for hope because of who God is:

> But this I call to mind,
>   and therefore I have hope:
>
> The steadfast love of the LORD never ceases;
>   his mercies never come to an end;
> they are new every morning;
>   great is your faithfulness.
> "The LORD is my portion," says my soul,
>   "therefore I will hope in him." (Lam. 3:21–24)

Do you see how God's love is steadfast and his mercies never end? The eternal God gives us himself as our portion. Our mortal minds cannot possibly comprehend the significance of such a gift.

When our children are struggling with separation anxiety, we give them reasons to have peace. When we, God's children, feel anxious that we are separated from him, he gives us indomitable cause to feel his peace.

The greatest demonstration of love that God has shown us is that he sent his Son, Jesus, to die in our place on the cross for our sins *while we were still his enemies* (Rom. 5:8). Jesus suffered the most profound "separation anxiety" that anyone in the world would ever face so that we who trust in him would always be joined to the Father forever. Although we were dead in our sins, God, being rich in mercy, loved us with such a great love that made us alive together with Christ by grace through faith (Eph. 2:4–8).

We'll never reach the end of the grace-filled implications of this brilliant gospel. Jonathan Edwards said, "Absolute sovereignty is what I love to ascribe to God."[26] I couldn't agree more—the sovereignty of God highlights the glorious freedom of God to lavish his grace on his enemies. A God who uses his freedom to save his enemies in such a way that ensures that they will be inexplicably rejoicing in him forever is a God who is worthy of all our worship. God's grace to us in Christ is greater than any frustration that threatens to unravel us. Because Jesus is upholding the universe with his word, we can trust him with any no-good, very bad day.

God's grace to us in Christ rescues us from idolizing motherhood. Because Jesus is supremely worthy of all our affections, there is no aspect of being a mom that can eclipse his beauty.

God's grace to us in Christ trumps our prideful self-delusions of "I've got everything under control." Because Jesus has authority over all things, we can joyfully humble ourselves under his merciful rule and serve him forever.

God's grace to us in Christ awakens our calloused, lethargic soul. Because Jesus's greatness is unsearchable, he is able to revive our lukewarm affections for him as we seek his face. There is but one great place where a mother can find out about the greatness of Jesus Christ: in God's word. Jerry Bridges advised: "Don't believe everything you think. You cannot be trusted to tell yourself the truth. Stay in the word."[27] J. I. Packer's recommendation is similar:

> Do I as a Christian understand myself ? Do I know my own real identity? My own real destiny? I am a child of God, God is my Father; heaven is my home; every day is one day nearer. My Saviour is my brother; every

Christian is my brother too. Say it over and over again to yourself first thing in the morning, last thing at night, as you wait for the bus, any time when your mind is free, and ask God that you may be enabled to live as one who knows it is all utterly and completely true. For this is the Christian's secret of the Christian life, of a God-honouring life.[28]

Steeping myself in God's word to discover the wonders of God's love toward me—a sinner—reminds me that I have no ground for boasting except in the cross of Jesus Christ (Gal. 6:14). These meditations serve to fuel my worship of Jesus, and inherent in that worship is a joy-driven telling of his faithfulness to all generations (Ps. 89:1). I want my children to "come with me" as I plumb the depths and height and breadth of the love of Christ.

The long view of motherhood sees far beyond the third trimester, potty training, and even high school graduation. The long view of motherhood scans the horizon of eternity. We understand that our child may one day be our brother or sister in Christ. We mothers always need to have the long view of life in our minds as we go about our days. God is about his work of creating people who are created and recreated in the image of his Son. We are part of the new humanity, a people whose pattern of life is being transformed by God so that we no longer walk in ways that enslave us in death and futility. The world will one day be filled with the glory of the Lord the way the waters cover the sea! In all our mothering, we look toward that day.

Maybe your day has just started, or it's well underway, or it's over and you're "in the time zones that are sleeping right now." No matter what time it is, it's a good time to give thanks to God for his rich mercies that are ever new to us through Jesus Christ and to share your joy with all who will listen.

Our calling as a mother is to press on with the strength that God supplies and make Jesus our own because he has made us his own (Phil. 3:12). We forget what lies behind, and we strain forward to what lies ahead, pressing on toward the goal for the prize of the upward call of God in Christ Jesus (Phil. 3:13–14).

You may have spent a great deal of thought in planning the first outfit in which you would dress your child when you brought her home. A few months ago friends of ours sent invitations for us to join them at the airport to help them welcome their adopted son into their family. Even more intentional and thoughtful than those things, the homecoming our heavenly Father has planned will absolutely blow our minds. As we treasure Christ in our motherhood, it causes us to be heavenly minded, thinking often of the Lord who has brought us into his forever family and empowering us to live for his kingdom as we serve our families.

———

Reflection

"The long view of motherhood scans the horizon of eternity," and holding that view is a fruit of the gospel. United to Christ, we learn to recognize grace at work in our lives and in the lives of our children—grace that's greater than frustration, grace that rescues us from mother idols, grace that strips the calluses off our souls and strengthens us to find all the joy God intended for motherhood.

1. We need to be reminded who God is every single day. How do we do that?

2. Unlike justification, which is applied to us just once for all time, sanctification—the process by which we are transformed into the image of Christ—is progressive. How does Romans 6:12–14 shine light on the process of sanctification?

3. Treasuring Christ is the key to discipleship. How do Jesus's parables of the hidden treasure and the pearl of great value (Matt. 13:44–46) speak to you as a mother? Look also at Matthew 7:19–24.

4. What perspective transforms your apathy and frustration (see Ps. 8:3–6; Eph. 1:22; and Col. 1:16)?

5. The prophet Jeremiah found hope in the midst of a frightening crisis, and his words of hope are recorded in Lamentations 3:21–24:

> But this I call to mind,
>   and therefore I have hope:

> The steadfast love of the LORD never ceases;
>   his mercies never come to an end;
> they are new every morning;
>   great is your faithfulness.
> "The LORD is my portion," says my soul,
>   "therefore I will hope in him."

What specific things do you see in this passage that led to Jeremiah's hope?

Going Deeper

Study the prayers of the apostle Paul in Ephesians 1:16–20 and 3:14–19. List the petitions in Paul's prayers. How do they differ from your regular petitions? Cultivate a habit of praying one or more of these petitions each day before you ask God to supply your temporal needs.

Notes

1. Herman Bavinck, *Reformed Dogmatics* (Grand Rapids, MI: Baker Academic, 2008), 3:455.
2. Martyn Lloyd-Jones, *Preaching and Preachers* (London: Hodder & Stoughton, 2012), 170–71.
3. The original quote is: "Don't ever degenerate into giving advice unconnected to the good news of Jesus crucified, alive, present, at work and returning." David Powlison, "Who Is God?," *Journal of Biblical Counseling* 17 (Winter 1999): 16.
4. Jeremiah Burroughs, *The Rare Jewel of Christian Contentment* (1650), http://www.monergism.com.
5. I'm indebted to Milton Vincent for pointing this out in his excellent book on treasuring the gospel, *A Gospel Primer for Christians: Learning to See the Glories of God's Love* (Bemidji, MN: Focus, 2008).
6. John Owen, *The Works of John Owen*, vol. 3, *The Holy Spirit* (Carlisle, PA: Banner of Truth, 1966), 100.
7. Richard Baxter, *The Practical Works of the Rev. Richard Baxter*, vol. 4 (London: Paternoster, 1830), 18.
8. Paul David Tripp, *Forever: Why You Can't Live without It* (Grand Rapids, MI: Zondervan, 2011), 141.

9. Joseph Hart, "Come, Ye Sinners, Poor and Needy," 1759.

10. This beloved tradition was inspired by Noël Piper's book *Most of All, Jesus Loves You!* (Wheaton, IL: Crossway, 2004).

11. Thomas Watson, *The Doctrine of Repentance*, ed. William Gross (On the Wing, 2011), 55, https://www.monergism.com.

12. John Piper, *Desiring God: Meditations of a Christian Hedonist* (Colorado Springs, CO: Multnomah, 2003), 12.

13. Thomas Chalmers, "The Expulsive Power of a New Affection," sermon, http://www.newble.co.uk/chalmers/comm9.html.

14. Edward Welch, *Running Scared: Fear, Worry, and the God of Rest* (Greensboro, NC: New Growth Press, 2007), 140.

15. Jerry Bridges, *The Discipline of Grace: God's Role and Our Role in the Pursuit of Holiness* (Colorado Springs, CO: Navpress, 2006), 19.

16. The publishing details for Jerry Bridges's book *The Discipline of Grace* can be found in note 15 above.

17. Vincent, *Gospel Primer for Christians*, 34.

18. John Bunyan, *Justification by an Imputed Righteousness*, https://acacia.pairsite.com/Acacia.John.Bunyan/.

19. Horatius Bonar, "God's Purpose of Grace," sermon, Kindle ed. (Chapel Library, August 23, 2018), loc. 149.

20. Sinclair Ferguson, *In Christ Alone: Living the Gospel-Centered Life* (Sanford, FL: Reformation Trust, 2007), 151.

21. Richard Sibbes, *Glorious Freedom* (Carlisle, PA: Banner of Truth, 2000), 81.

22. Sibbes, *Glorious Freedom*, 83.

23. Bavinck, *Reformed Dogmatics*, 3:455.

24. Sibbes, *Glorious Freedom*, 91–92.

25. Owen, *Works of John Owen*, 108–9.

26. Jonathan Edwards, *Selections* (New York: Hill and Wang, 1962), 58–59.

27. Jerry Bridges, *The Great Exchange: My Sin for His Righteousness* (Wheaton, IL: Crossway, 2007).
28. J. I. Packer, *Knowing God* (Downers Grove, IL: InterVarsity Press, 2011), 259.

Scripture Index

Scripture Index

Also Available from Gloria Furman

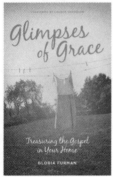

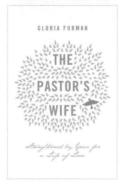

For more information, visit **crossway.org**.